A Poetic
Ministree, Inc.

I HAD TO DIE EXPOSING WITCHCRAFT IN THE CHURCH

By

Evelyn Murray Drayton

Prophetess Heddie Simmons
May the hand of God continue
to rest upon you!

Evelyn M. Drayton
Oct. 27, 2004

authorHOUSE

A Poetic Ministree, Inc.

1663 Liberty Drive, Suite 200
Bloomington, Indiana 47403
(800) 839-8640
www.authorhouse.com

© 2004 Evelyn Murray Drayton
All Rights Reserved.

No part of this book may be reproduced, stored in a retrieval system, or transmitted by any means without the written permission of the author.

First published by AuthorHouse 06/25/04

ISBN: 1-4184-2021-2 (sc)

Library of Congress Control Number: 2004094920

Printed in the United States of America
Bloomington, Indiana

This book is printed on acid-free paper.

Unless otherwise indicated, all scripture quotations are taken from the King James Version of The New Open Bible (1990). Nashville, TN: Thomas Nelson, Inc.

ACKNOWLEDGEMENT

I would like to thank my husband, Russell, for his patience while I worked on this book. Sometimes I became frustrated because it seemed as if he was not interested in my project. Nevertheless, I finally saw it from his point of view and understood that he wanted me to really take my time with this project and be confident in the direction in which the Lord was leading me. Because of Russell's encouragement, I was able to put the manuscript aside and really search myself to be sure that the purpose of this book is to help someone else and not to defame anyone's character nor to promote self. In this way, I was able to crucify self and die a little bit more.

Melissa, thanks for your timely assistance.

Table of Contents

Preface ix

Introduction xi

Chapter One
    Dying Means You Are Experiencing Growth 1

Chapter Two
    Struggles Within My Own Walls 13

Chapter Three
    My Children Were Used by God to Help Me Grow 23

Chapter Four
    My Secular Job Prepared Me For My Ministry 29

Chapter Five
    God Changed Rules To Fulfill A Prophecy 39

Chapter Six
    My Encounter With Witchcraft And False Prophecy 49

Chapter Seven
    Another Sister Shares Her Encounter With Witchcraft 85

Chapter Eight
    The Battle Is Never For Nothing 91

Chapter Nine
    Spiritual Death Is Imminent When The Spirit Lives 97

Chapter Ten
    Real Living Comes After You Have Died (Spiritually) 105

Chapter Eleven
    Guess Who Helps To Certify Your Death 109

Chapter Twelve
    Living During Suffering Season 113

Chapter Thirteen
    Scriptures That Helped Me To Win My Battle 119

Chapter Fourteen
    Some Important Things I Learned During My Suffering 127

Conclusion 133

PREFACE

This book was birthed as a result of a witchcraft experience that I encountered in a church. A church leader told me that if I told what had happened at this one particular prayer service, he would preach my funeral in 90 days. Yes, I died; but I did not die a physical death like that leader and a false prophetess wanted me to die. Instead, I died to my flesh daily—I died God's way! This book is not intended to defame anyone's character, but merely to inform people of the craftiness of Satan and to manifest the power of God in the lives of his people. It is hoped that the information and testimonies included in this book enlighten you and give you strength on your Christian journey.

INTRODUCTION

As you begin to relax and read this book, I will salute you by using Paul's greeting in Colossians 1:2 when he said, "…Grace be unto you, and peace, from God our Father and the Lord Jesus Christ" and pray you receive a blessing as you read to the glory and honor of God.

The purpose of this book is to give honor and praise to my Father, God, by showing to man through my life experiences that God is in full control and is all-powerful. I did not prepare this book with "enticing words of man's wisdom" (I Corinthians 2:4). I want all men to know that God is still a Savior and a Mighty Deliverer. In order to manifest the power of God through our lives, it is necessary that situations arise so that God has an opportunity to prove His power. These situations prepare us to go through a growth process and help us develop a stable relationship with the Lord so that He can use us to manifest His power to the fullest.

This is my true story of how I faced various issues in my life as related to my spiritual walk with the Lord. My trials and triumphs have truly become a part of my message and my tests yielded the fruit of my testimonies. Through my struggles, I can now tell dying men and women everywhere that they can live if they are willing to die for the sake of Jesus Christ. I am taking advantage of my trials and am using my crises to tell others about Jesus the Christ. Satan will try to trick you into believing that you have reached the end of your rope and that your life is over when certain difficulties arise. Don't give in to such deceptive words of the enemy. Please know that your deliverance may be just around the bend.

In August 2001 being inspired by the Holy Spirit, I testified at a church that the Lord had allowed me to experience so many things in life that one day I would write a book to share some of my experiences. At the time of my testimony, I did not expect the subsequent supplementary chapters in my life about the confrontation with witchcraft later the same year.

About a year after my church testimony, a long-time friend from out of town prophesied to me saying, "God said you are to write a book." I looked at my friend and smiled. The prophecy from my friend was not a surprise to me. It was, however, a timely confirmation from the Lord for me to get busy. You see, my friend did not know about my testimony at church, nor had I mentioned anything about the book. Amazingly, I knew that I was 'dragging my feet' and that God had just sent me a wake-up call through my friend to get busy.

I yearn to make a difference in my life and in the lives of others. Now I know that writing this book can make that difference in someone's life. God gave me the title of this book one Saturday night while lying on my bed meditating. I want it known that this book is birthed through much suffering, betrayal, pain, and rejection. Even so, my spiritual death struggle is not all about me; it is about God.

It is hoped that you are encouraged to believe that just as I overcame situations in my life, you also can make it through whatever comes your way in life. If you are determined to see Jesus, He will see you through. To God are the power, the glory, and the honor.

Chapter One
Dying Means You Are Experiencing Growth

Dying Means You Are Experiencing Growth

"As newborn babes, desire the sincere milk of the word, that ye may grow thereby…" (I Peter 2:2)

    As I look back over my life, I can see where God has used some of the most unusual things in life to teach me great lessons. One of the greatest lessons I have ever learned is that <u>Christians can't grow and produce fruit until they die</u>. I had to die in order to grow spiritually.

    When individuals grow spiritually, those persons actually die from things in their lives that would prevent them from obeying and enjoying the presence of God. This flesh does not want to obey God, and therefore, we must kill this flesh so that the Spirit of God reigns and rules in our lives. I want to be in God's presence; therefore, I had to die.

    You may ponder the question about my spiritual preparation and ability to do spiritual warfare before I encountered the witchcraft experience that I will discuss later. Before I was able to battle with witchcraft, I had earlier long-term growth experiences. You see, we don't become spiritual warriors overnight nor do we become spiritual heroines or giant slayers as a result of one trial.

I found out that just as there are different stages of physical growth there are also stages of spiritual growth. The stages of growth I used for comparison was that of my own physical growth. I know there were times when I needed someone to feed me, clean me, clothe me, protect me, etc. I know there were times when I could not talk, crawl, walk, or run. Even those who nurtured and cared for me expected growth in my life. No one expects a baby to remain in the infant stage forever—right?

Spiritually, I had to go through a growth process. Second Corinthians 5:17 tells us: "Therefore if any man be in Christ, he is a new creature: old things are passed away; behold all things are become new." So, when I accepted Christ as Savior, I had to start off as a new creature. This step is considered the baby step (I Peter 2:2). The process of spiritual growth and development had now begun.

I needed to be fed, cleaned, clothed, etc. I also had to learn how to talk, crawl, walk, and run. I went through these stages physically, and I had to go through the same stages spiritually. I had to grow up.

You know what? I found out that the growing process takes time. I also found out that it was spiritually unhealthy to expect drastic changes overnight. Paul said in First Corinthians 13:11, "When I was a child, I spake as a child, I understood as a child, I thought as a child: but when I became a man, I put away childish things." No one ever born became a man overnight; however, over time you notice the difference and the result of growth. Spiritually, **Which stage are you in right now? Are you a baby, a man/woman, or somewhere in between?** Do you need some help answering those questions? Hint: Think about things that babies do: whimper, fuss, etc. about almost any and everything. But not for a man/woman, not a real man/woman!

It seems I wanted to grow spiritually, but I did not like the growth process. I detested the times when I had to learn things the hard way. I resisted the fact when I learned that I had to DIE in order to grow. By dying, I mean learning and practicing the ways of God rather than obeying and yielding to my fleshly desires. I had heard about "growing in the Lord." But no one ever taught me that I had to die in order to grow spiritually.

I recently listened to an eight-tape cassette series entitled *Spiritual Growth in Christian Education* by Dr. Steve Lowe, a professor at Erskine Theological Seminary in Due West, South Carolina where I attended during Fall 2003. Dr. Lowe's assignment required each student to select a main point from the tapes and then write a report about that main point. It is amazing how God chose one main point out of the entire eight-tape series to have such a tremendous impact on my life.

Dr. Lowe says, "We MUST go through a process of growth. We must go through an orderly, sequential, step by step process of growth." I don't think I will ever forget those words because until I heard those words from Dr. Lowe, I thought my struggles and troubles, including the witchcraft experience that I will share later, were all about me. Profoundly, I learned that it was not a personal attack on me after all. Strikingly, it was about my spiritual growth and development and becoming the person whom I need to be in order to adequately represent the Kingdom of God. I just know without a doubt that God used these few words from a taped lecture to give me an answer for which I had been searching for years.

Dr. Lowe's tape series taught me that when we confess that we are Christians, we enter a spiritual growth process and begin to experience changes that last for our entire life span. It is not effective to soul winning for the body of Christ to only speak of changes in our lives as Christians. We must be honest with ourselves and realize that we must also show the life changes that we talk about.

All children do not develop at the same pace so we should not expect all Christians to grow at the same level within the same time frame. With this truth in mind, we should not be so quick to judge our sister or brother when comparing levels of spiritual maturity. Time may not necessarily bring about the change, but given enough time, the world should be able to see changes in one's spiritual growth and development based on the individual's daily decisions.

The Christian life and spiritual walk can be compared to teachers who want their students to not only give answers for math problems but also show their work. In the same way, we must show our growth to the world as we grow up and develop in the things of God. We can clearly display our various stages of growth by the way we present ourselves to the world.

Dr. Lowe responded to one of my earlier assignments by saying that the "nature of the growth process is 'episodic' and 'seasonal'. There are periods of plateau and leveling off. Then there are spurts of growth that are not only observed by you but by others as well. They can therefore 'imitate you as you imitate Christ.' This is the power of the Body at work!"

After reading Dr. Lowe's comments, I recalled a period in my life when I recognized a big spurt in my spiritual growth as a result of a traumatic crisis. I can say that I experienced many referenced stages (ups, downs, spurts) of faith. Due to experiencing the various stages, I am now able to speak boldly about God's Word and His power. I can boldly tell others that God rewards us when we obey His Word. I can also tell others that the Holy Spirit still speaks to us and gives us direction and guidance for our lives if only we would listen. I have definitely matured spiritually through the crises in my life.

The learning process for me appeared to be a long one. Nevertheless, I finally learned that I had to be stretched in order for me to grow spiritually. My stretching, for some reason, came through much pain. It seems I experienced some degree of pain, though not always physical, through each phase of growth in my life. Consequently, if my crises were necessary for me to be the person that I am today, and I believe they were, then I am most grateful for the experiences.

My growth was pending on my actions and reactions to my crises. God, in His infinite wisdom and time, allowed me to endure and learn from my challenging and diversified experiences. Now, as a result of not aborting the growth steps in my life, I am more prepared and equipped spiritually to fulfill my purpose in life.

Now that I know my crises were inevitable and were ordained by God as a part of my growth experience, I treasure those critical periods in my life. From a spiritual baby's standpoint, it seems I would have taken an alternate route for my life by eliminating my pains. However, proxy can never teach the "orderly, sequential, and step by step" growth experiences designed specifically for my life. I, and I alone, must fulfill every plan that has been ordained for my life.

Please keep in mind that all Christians need spiritual nourishment in order to grow and develop. The best nourishment that I know of is the Word of God. Bible reading and meditation were critical for my growth. "As newborn babes, desire the sincere milk of the word, that ye may grow thereby…" (I Peter 2:2). I read the Bible more during hard times in life than at any other times in my life. I had to learn, however, that I needed to study the Word prior to the hard times. I had to learn how to apply the Word of God to my daily decisions.

Just as Bible reading and meditation are important for growth and development, prayer is necessary for spiritual growth and development. We cannot afford to pray only during crises. We must pray during our days of strengths and weaknesses because they can be used to help us obtain a better relationship with God and rely on Him even more. The thing we initially identify as a weakness could very well end up being our strength.

During my growth process, I found myself praying for other people. Sometimes I would know that other things were on my prayer agenda but the Holy Spirit urged me to pray for others—even those who had talked about me or criticized me. In the early days, I couldn't fully understand it all when I acquired the urge to pray for other people. I would just call their names and ask God to extend His mercy. I do thank God for loving people so much that He allows others to intercede on their behalf. We must always remember that our Christian walk is not all about us but is also about those who live around us.

Forgiveness is also a necessary ingredient for growth and development. The Word of God helps us to forgive those who have wronged us. I had to practice forgiveness and reinforce it in my heart time and time again because of the damages I received from others. Still I know I have never suffered by being nailed to a cross like Jesus. At the same time Jesus was suffering, He asked the Father to forgive the people who were crucifying Him on the cross. So, although I have experienced some things and am still experiencing things, I have learned that forgiveness is imperative for spiritual growth. Matthew 6:12-15 teach us about forgiveness "And forgive us our debts, as we forgive our debtors…For if ye forgive men their trespasses, your heavenly Father will also forgive you: But if ye forgive not men their trespasses, neither will your Father forgive your trespasses."

Through all I had already experienced, another major crisis developed in my life. This major crisis involved witchcraft. (I will discuss this more fully later). I came to a point where I questioned my spiritual maturity because this witchcraft experience caused me to experience shame, guilt, doubt, and even confusion. I experienced shame because pride had me thinking that nothing so painful could ever happen to me, a child of God. I experienced guilt because other people had me thinking that I was the one who contributed to mayhem in my life. I experienced doubt because I kept asking if God was with me in this situation. And finally, I experienced confusion at times when I tried to remedy the situation using man's way versus God's way. Man was telling me how I "ought to" handle my situation but I was hearing God's Word telling me the opposite way. Though I questioned some things, I knew that I was mature enough to choose to obey and do things God's way.

Obedience is a great asset during growth and development. Many people questioned some of the decisions that I made during the witchcraft experience. One big decision, for example, was refusing to seek revenge against those who had wronged me. I knew that various scriptures taught me that vengeance belongs to God. Psalm 37:12-13 say, "The wicked plotteth against the just, and gnasheth upon him with his teeth. The Lord shall laugh at him: for he seeth that his day is coming." Matthew 6:4 tells us, "…and thy Father which seeth in secret himself shall reward thee openly." I had to obey the Word and trust God to work things out in my life. I obeyed God, and though I did not see immediate results, I am victorious in the end!

I recognized when frustration and fury were at an all time high in my life; I could have compromised my relationship with the Lord, and exemplified some not so godly actions. But I say to you, don't compromise the Holy Spirit on the inside of you for any reason. Critical times such as I experienced in my life can reveal growth and development.

God knows your needs, how to meet your needs, and when to meet your needs, etc. Matthew 6:33 tells us to "…seek ye first the kingdom of God, and his righteousness; and all these things shall be added unto you." So, don't compromise your relationship with God by any means, for anyone, for anything, anywhere, at anytime. That is just how important and how valuable your relationship is with God. Paul says in Galatians 2:20, "I am crucified with Christ: nevertheless I live; yet not I but Christ liveth in me: and the life which I now live in the flesh I live by the faith of the Son of God, who loved me, and gave himself for me."

We cannot afford to try to preach, witness, and serve God without experiencing some growth and development. A growth process is necessary in order to become the changed, responsible servant that God is seeking. A servant of God, because of continuous growth and development, is equipped to be of service to others. A minister once told me "We don't work for the church, we <u>serve</u> the church."

As a means of service, I mentally placed myself on a heavenly job. I first set up God's headquarters in heaven. I chose Jesus as my earthly supervisor and Holy Spirit as my co-worker who works along with me to accomplish my task. Then I quietly asked God to let His kingdom rule on earth as I serve the church on earth in obedience to Christ, my supervisor. Of course, I had to learn the hard way that on-the-job training (growth and development) is a requirement for heavenly promotions. What a wonderful, heavenly privilege that I have to work on earth and receive heavenly benefits! My spiritual growth and development definitely means more than this world to me.

Yes, I am learning to die daily from things that would hinder me from having a relationship with my Savior. Jesus died for me to give me His anointing. I want to die for Jesus so that I can receive his anointing and keep it. I want to protect my relationship with Him. When my anointing is to be compromised, I can stand boldly and say, NO WAY, because I had to DIE to get this anointing. And you know what…you really have to die in order to get it and KEEP it.

Therefore, I <u>want to die</u> and dying then becomes easier the closer you walk with God. You must realize what a treasure you have on the inside of you and strive daily to walk with God. It is not necessarily your doing, doing, doing that pleases God but may I suggest that it is by your dying day after day, after day.

Dying is all about choices we make in obeying God while the flesh is being crucified. It is such a great and exciting day in one's life when one has gone through tribulation and has overcome a great trial successfully. You would not want to exchange what you learned during the testing for anything because nothing else compares to the things for which you suffered in order to yield fruitful end results. "But the God of all grace, who hath called us unto his eternal glory by Christ Jesus, after that ye hath suffered a while, make you perfect, stablish, strengthen, settle you" (I Peter 5:10). All things really do work out for your good in fulfillment of God's plan.

Yes, I NEEDED to die because I NEEDED to grow. I had to really learn how to trust and depend on Jesus for progress in my growth and developmental stages. And amazingly, I grew and developed by dying to this flesh. I did not die a physical death the way a church leader and a false prophetess wanted me to die (I will discuss this later). Instead, I died to my flesh daily—I died God's way day after day, after day!

Chapter Two
Struggles Within
My Own Walls

Struggles Within
My Own Walls

Although there were changes in my life as a result of my growing stages, I had struggles within my own walls, not just church people to deal with. I had struggles against walls within (myself) and without (other people).

When my husband, Russell, and I would have disagreements, I would read some negative comments back to him that he told me a few days earlier. Oh yes, I had most of his negative comments in writing, because for a while, I considered him one of my obstacles (walls).

One day when I was REALLY frustrated, I told Russell that I was keeping record of all the negative things he had said to me. Then he asked me whether I was recording any of the negative things that I had done and said to him. Even though I was upset with him at the time and considered him "a wall", his words were like a mirror to me and I was convicted. Suddenly, I retrieved my note pad and started reading over some of my notes; and sure enough, I had recorded some of the "special" good things that I had said to Russell.

In addition, I read First Corinthians Chapter 13, where the Word tells me that love keeps no record of wrongdoing. So yes, the Lord used the situation between Russell and me to get me to see who I really was and what I was doing. Yes, I had a wall "within" and I had to die from it. I saw that there were, indeed, some things inside of me that I had to die from in order to please God. And yes, I had struggles within my walls that I had to contend with for a while; but I had to confront walls without while I live with walls within. The enemy meant my walls for evil, but God used the situation between Russell and me to make me a better person and helped me to see the superior qualities that I had overlooked in my husband.

Well, I must admit that when I moved to Georgetown, I didn't want anyone to know that I had been called into the ministry and had actually been licensed to preach even before I got married. Russell declared if he knew before we got married that I was a minister, he probably wouldn't have married me. Through it all, though, God brought about a change. I had to change MY negative attitude and tear down the wall I had built for my husband. God, through changes I made in my life, opened a door for Him to deal with Russell. Though my husband initially resisted my ministry, he is now supporting my ministry greatly.

To give a brief summary about my early ministry before I moved to Georgetown, those were some difficult and trying days for me. I accepted Christ on October 18, 1975, and began early ministry training by serving in the capacities of church janitor, church announcer, Sunday school teacher, usher, choir member, musician (I banged the drums and the keyboard), and last, but not least, served as a licensed minister. Yes, I was a licensed preacher before I even moved to Georgetown. You might ask the question, "Why didn't she want people to know that she was a preacher?" Well, I am glad you asked. Despite all of this previous training and spiritual exposure, in my opinion, I still failed as a Christian. You see popularity has nothing to do with your spirituality. Yes, I had positions in the church; yet secretly, I was living a different life style contrary to that as a representative of Christ. Again, I learned the hard way that nothing or no one can fill the void designated for the Holy Spirit. I saw the spiritual "rut" that I was in as a result of slipping and sliding into sin.

I didn't want to be a stumbling block to anyone else in the church so I requested that I vacate the pulpit until I felt spiritually strong enough to resist the sins that led to my downfall. My request was graciously granted; but at the same time, I stayed before God in prayer. Changes were made in my life over time and I was invited back to the pulpit. I was so humbled and honored to occupy the pulpit again, but in my heart I was afraid of failure AGAIN and I did all I could to find excuses not to preach. Yes, I experienced a lot in my early ministry. I had some good days and I had some bad days but all of those days of experiences helped me to be the woman that I am today.

After I moved to Georgetown, South Carolina in 1987, as a licensed minister, I wanted to start all over again. I told myself that the last thing I need to do is tell people that I am a preacher because it seemed that would have been so much pressure on me to prove myself. I felt that maybe if no one knew that I was a preacher maybe I could just sing and testify during worship service and that would suffice. I would often feel the power and presence of God as I prayed and testified in church and said, "Yes, Lord, I'll do what you want me to do." In a way, I was glad that I had not yet told anybody that I was called to preach. In this new city of Georgetown, I figured people would be able to observe my life style, observe the way I walked and talked, and could see that God had His hand on me, without having a label as a minister. For this reason I am glad I didn't announce my ministry too early.

Then it seems Satan continued to silence me and I started using guilt to suppress my testimony even though God had already forgiven me. I began to say that there was no way possible that I could still be used by God to preach after all I had allowed to happen in my life before and even after I met my husband. I didn't feel God could use me anymore and I didn't want people to have high expectations or anything of me. I didn't want to bring any shame to the name of Jesus because of my past or present situation. But a few times, God allowed different ministers to prophesy publicly and said something like "God is going to use this young lady greatly in the ministry." You know what—when God allows a seed such as that to be planted in one's heart, Satan tries to steal the seed immediately after it is planted.

Despite hearing the various prophecies over my life about ministry, I had allowed myself to set up several defense mechanisms to cope with this situation and other problems that I was facing. While these defense mechanisms may have served my purpose for a while, I felt I could not continue lying to myself. I had to admit that I needed a closer walk with my

Savior. I finally repented to God AGAIN, forgave myself, got over my guilt and shame, and continued to ask God to use me.

I did not have to wait until another human tell me I was doing wrong—the Holy Spirit Himself convicted me of sin in my life. When the Holy Spirit convicts you, you must acknowledge your sin, repent, and forsake those ways that displease God. One must truly repent from the heart and not just from the lips. If you don't repent from the heart, you will find yourself committing the same sin until you are in bondage. And believe me, temptations will always be available to keep you in bondage because Satan knows your weaknesses.

I learned the hard way that changes are necessary in order to develop and exemplify the lifestyle and examples that Jesus Christ left for us to follow. I guess admitting my bondage was one of the times that I had to move to a different level of growth. I needed to learn going through trials with the right attitude will allow us to emerge as a stronger, wiser, and a more empowered person.

It amazes me now, though, to see how the body of Christ allows so many fleshly things in the ministry these days, including witchcraft. Most ministers can do anything they want to a congregation, live any lifestyle, etc. and there doesn't seem to be any remorse anywhere. These same ministers who may be reported for wrong doings by their congregations are sometimes quietly moved to a BIGGER and BETTER church as a form of reprimand—if enough people from the congregation squeal loud enough for a change. Anyhow, I just thought I would interject that quick thought of frustration because I love God's house, the place where His honor should abide.

When I settled in Georgetown, I felt a little like Abraham whom God told to move from among his kinsfolk. I now know why God moved me to Georgetown and how He was preparing me to be blessed and at the same time be a blessing to others. I FINALLY got the nerve to go and share with my husband about my spiritual struggle and how I had to obey God with my ministry. I asked my husband a few times if it was all right with him if I applied for my evangelist license in a new denomination. On each occasion, Russell would tell me, "No." He even told me one time that the more I got involved with religion the less attractive I became to him. Did I cry? Emphatically. Did I have second thoughts about my ministry? Categorically, I must admit I did. Did I love the Lord enough to dry my tears and say, "Lord, I still love you and I still want to obey you?" Yes, I did. I believe God allowed Russell to say all of these things to me for my good so that I could be sure whether or not I really want to be in ministry. After hearing all of that negative feedback, I could have given up and said it wasn't worth it. But I thank God for the strength to be able to eat and digest things that the average person probably wouldn't dare swallow. According to Second Chronicles 32:31, God left Hezekiah alone for a while "to try him, that he might know all that was in his heart." Having read that scripture, I searched my relationship with God and myself and was confident I was walking in God's will—although Russell kept telling me "no."

Sure enough, when Russell was stricken with cancer in October 1999, I asked him <u>one more time</u> if I could apply for my minister's license.

(God had already revealed to me during prayer that Russell's sickness was not unto death and that he would be a blessing to my ministry). Amiably, he told me to go ahead and that he did not want to stand in my way. He said that he expressed some of those negative feelings toward me earlier because it seemed our lifestyles would clash: the conflict being that he is a motorcycle enthusiast and I am a minister. Russell also told me later that he had seen a moral weakening among some ministers and that he just didn't want to see his wife caught up in the pandemonium. I love him for expressing that sincere concern for me.

Through all I experienced with Russell and my ministry, I saw God take a potential setback and brought forth good to accomplish His purpose. Shortly after I received my husband's favorable response, I applied for and received my license to preach from a denomination other than the one of which I was formerly licensed. (The main point I wanted to stress here is that although I had heard from God about my ministry, I wanted to respect my husband and have his blessing). Approximately two years after being licensed, I was ordained as an itinerant minister in the same denomination —just as God had revealed it to me.

Russell, one whom I thought at one time to be one of my worst critics, and a wall, is really a gauge in my life to help me accomplish my purpose in life. All of his critique helps me to be a better wife, preacher, and friend. I don't ever ask him specific questions if I am not ready to hear the truth for an answer. He looks me straight in the eyes and tells me exactly how he feels, point blank. My husband said to me one day after I accepted a speaking engagement over the telephone: "Don't look for me to follow you around every time you accept a preaching engagement because God didn't call me to preach; you said He called you." I looked at him half hurt and half ecstatic! Much to my surprise, however, Russell has been very supportive and has traveled with me on numerous speaking engagements. As a matter of fact, he has traveled with me at times when I least expected him to.

After listening to Dr. Lowe's tape lecture, *Spiritual Growth in Christian Education*, I know now that my experiences were necessary for my life and that I could not skip my ordained "orderly, sequential, step by step process of growth." I also had to learn the hard way that even though a person may be anointed for a special service, the individual still has to go through a period of training or testing in order to be properly equipped for spiritual battle.

Naturally, I believe we as Christians must be guided and equipped in order to grow and develop into the end product destined for our lives. Nonetheless, there are many who can learn from the experiences of other Christians. But, there are some of us who are determined to learn things the hard way—our own way. For some strange reason, I was one of those persons, it seemed, destined to make my own path. But, I am learning now, that there are forerunners who are willing to be a blessing and share some of their life experiences—just as I am doing in this book.

As a forerunner, I am sure that I have hurt people unintentionally; and likewise, people have hurt me. Family, friends, and foes, alike, have talked about me, belittled me, betrayed me, and even deceived me. Yet, I am learning to march forward into battle to be who God has called me to be and fulfill my purpose. Now that I have gone through a rigorous process of training and dying, I am now a happy, well equipped, ordained itinerant minister AND <u>I HAVE</u> Russell's Blessing to be in public ministry.

You see, God knows all about our future, and if we obey, God will work on our behalf. God was preparing me for future battles as I demolished walls in my life through obedience to Him and in submission to my husband. I will show you later how God took all of my preceding experiences to prepare me for greater battles. So, how was I prepared to do warfare with the spirit of witchcraft? I learned the hard way, that's how!! By this, I mean that former battles, hurts, pains, and disappointments forced me to my knees to seek the strength, help, and mercy of God.

Wow! God is so faithful that He will not give you an assignment then turn around and lock all the doors so you can't complete the assignment. "…Whatsoever he saith unto you, do it" (John 2:5). He knows what He is doing!!

I can truly stand on Romans 8:28, which says "And we know that all things work together for good to them that love God, to them who are the called according to his purpose." I am seeing my walls fall every day—within and without—because I am learning to die. GOD STILL HAD A PLAN.

Chapter Three
My Children Were Used by God to Help Me Grow

My Children
Were Used by God to Help Me Grow

It appears to me that my children are sometimes used to show me how God's children behave spiritually. I believe if you ask a mother who has more than one child, she will tell you that each child behaves differently. I believe the same stands true for God's spiritual children.

I have even compared my discipline techniques in the natural to the way God chastises and disciplines me as His child in the supernatural. I really do find similarities most of the times. Hebrews 12:5-11 tell us that God chastises His children and that we are to "…DESPISE NOT THOU THE CHASTENING OF THE LORD, NOR FAINT WHEN THOU ART REBUKED OF HIM: FOR WHOM THE LORD LOVETH HE CHASTENETH…"

Anyhow, I have seen times when God used my children to teach me lessons about my spiritual journey. God does use children to help accomplish his purpose, you know. Psalm 8:2 declares, "Out of the mouth of babes and sucklings hast thou ordained strength…" So, I can truly thank God for my children because they have taught me a lot.

My two boys (Justin and Nicholas) were used by God sometimes to help teach me as well as encourage me from time to time about spiritual matters. For example, sometimes I would be pondering a question in my mind. My boys would come around me, for some strange reason, and say something or ask me a question concerning the very same question for which I was seeking an answer from God. The strange thing is that they would give me parts of the answer by the way they ask me their question, etc., not even knowing what I was thinking about.

I can recall a period when both of the boys had cold symptoms and I gave them some bitter but potent medication. They both got well in a reasonable time, I suppose. Well, within the next few days it seems I was under the weather with the same symptoms of which the boys had just recovered.

When the boys detected that I was sick, the two of them had conspired to give me the same bitter medicine that I had given them. They said "Come on, Mommy, take your medicine so you can feel better." Though I was not feeling well, I smiled at them and said, "Boys, that medicine is for children. Save it for the next time the two of you are sick." They insisted that they were not going to leave me in that bed sick while medicine was in my room. After all, they needed me to get better and help take care of them. Well, I told them that Daddy (Russell) would take good care of them. Still they were persistent. So, I finally took a little bit of the medicine just so they would let me rest.

Oh, my goodness, that medicine taste nasty! When the boys saw that sour look on my face, they both laughed, and I did too! They laughed and said, "Now, you got a dose of your own nasty medicine." The boys made me laugh so much; I actually forgot that I was sick. But you know what, I learned at lot from that occurrence. I learned that we must be careful what we say and what we do to others because the same bitter medicine that we administer to others may be the very dosage that we have to swallow later on. After all, "we will reap what we sow" (Galatians 6:7).

One other special occurrence stays in my mind, this one may sound weird, but it's true! When I was employed with the public utility company out of town, I worked with various budgets but most emphasis was placed on the Operations and Maintenance (O&M) Budget. I was at home one evening praying alone, diligently, that my department did not exceed the budget because there were some outstanding emergency expenses that I did not include in the year-end projections that I submitted to my boss. I mean I was on hands and knees crying out to God. When I heard my husband and the boys drive up, I immediately got off my knees and sat on the couch as if I was only reading a book.

My boys came in the house ahead of my husband. My oldest son (Justin) came in the house first and looked at me and said "Mommy, why is there an 'O' and an 'M' on the left side of your face. I said, "what?" I got a chill all over my body. I know that he couldn't have heard my prayer because they had just pulled up in the driveway. Anyhow, I discreetly felt my face, but I couldn't <u>feel</u> anything out of the ordinary or that was unusual. Then my youngest son (Nicholas) came into the house a few minutes later.

Justin then immediately told Nicholas to look at my face and tell him what he saw. Then Nicholas said the same identical thing that Justin said without any collaboration between the two of them. Then I told Nicholas to put his finger on Mommy's face indicating where the letters "O" and "M" were. He came straight to me and put his finger on my left cheek. I burst out in tears and thanked God for hearing my prayer and confirming His favorable response to my prayer request. I then explained to the boys that I had been praying about my company's O&M budget (they didn't know about O&M budgets but they tied the "O" and "M" to what I was saying) and I continued to tell them how real God is to Mommy. The boys shared this incident with my husband as soon as he entered the house.

When I went to work the next day I told my boss I was confident that we were going to end the year in the black. Sure enough, when I received my year-end numbers some time later, the numbers were better than I had anticipated. That may seem like a small matter to some of you, but not to me.

On another occasion, I jumped out of bed one morning—rushing, rushing, and rushing—and didn't even say my prayers. I thought I could get away with it for just a little while and just started doing what I thought I needed to get done. You know without prayer, it seems my day just didn't start off right. It seems I was not making any progress. As I was sitting in my den, I tried to figure out what was wrong with me. My son Nicholas came up to me and said "Mommy, just start over." He then went into another room and started playing as if he didn't say anything. My eyes were opened as the Holy Spirit had used my child to get my attention. I thought about what

Nicholas said and I then said, "Yes, Lord, I will start over and I will start with prayer." I fell on my knees and prayed. Oh, what joy filled my soul and my day went well!

You may wonder what those incidents involving my children have to do with my spiritual growing and dying. It is all right for you to question this and I don't mind responding. Well, I can sum it all in a few words. Momentous occurrences that I experienced with my children made me trust and depend on God's faithfulness even more. Yes, my children were used to help me die to self and learn the ways of God.

I died in more ways than one when I talked about my children. In fact, when I would try to testify in church about such occurrences, some would look at me as if I were stupid and it seems they wanted me to shut up. This made me die a little bit more.

As a result, I am more attuned to the ways in which God's Holy Spirit moves. God is a loving Father and He is SO good. Isn't it great that we can go to Him with all of our heart's concerns! (I will tell you later how Satan tried to destroy my children through witchcraft). AGAIN, GOD HAD A PLAN!

Chapter Four
My Secular Job Prepared Me For My Ministry

My Secular Job Prepared Me For My Ministry

I have had several jobs in my lifetime and I have actually learned something about my life from each of those former jobs. I recall my first permanent job in 1975 as a teacher's aide in Summerton, South Carolina. When I applied for that job, I did not have a vehicle, so I had to walk between ten to twelve miles from home and then caught a ride the rest of the way to submit my job application—that's how bad I wanted a job. I was hired and worked as a teacher's aide for several years and was later promoted to school secretary. Through this employment, I was able to earn nine years of service towards retirement.

I was attending a technical college at night while employed with the school system. After I obtained my associate degree at night, I left employment to attend a four-year college full time. While I was in college, I worked several part-time jobs to help pay my bills (Yes, I had a vehicle by now and you know what bills go along with owning a vehicle). Through my part-time employment, I was able to earn another year of service toward my retirement while I was in college. At this point though, I had very little money and decided to withdraw funds that I had contributed to the retirement system. After I had filled out all the paperwork and was ready to sign on the dotted line, I was interrupted by the district bookkeeper. The district bookkeeper begged me not to withdraw the funds. She said one day I will be glad if I would only listen to her wisdom. With less than $25 in my checking account at the time, I walked away in obedience to her request and tore up my paperwork. Only by the grace of God were my financial needs met. Nevertheless, I thank God this very day that I listened to that bookkeeper. (I will tell you why later).

I endured the financial struggle and obtained my Bachelor of Science Degree in Business Administration with an emphasis in accounting. After I obtained my bachelors degree, I still didn't find a good job locally. So, the Holy Spirit directed me to move from my hometown to a place where I knew no one. (I felt like brother Abraham in the book of Genesis). The Lord directed me to Georgetown, South Carolina where I landed a secretarial position with an opportunity for advancement. I contemplated the move to the new job and said, "Lord, are you having me to move that far to work as a secretary?" But, wait, GOD HAD A PLAN.

In a little over a year, with God's help and the help of newly acquired friends, I applied for and was hired for an accounting position with the same company out of town. It seems none of my former jobs prepared me for my ministry the way my jobs at this public utility company prepared me for my future ministry. It was a challenge for me to accept the secretarial job; but it was an even greater challenge to accept the accounting position out of town and commute so far away from home. My husband really did not want me driving 64 miles one way to work. But, he noticed my determination and eventually agreed for me to accept the job. God was so good; He even allowed my husband to purchase another reliable car for me to take the long commute. Undeniably, I knew the Holy Spirit was directing me and strategically planting me at the new job. Despite this fact, privately, I fussed and told the Lord how hard I had worked all my life and fussed about the distance to my new job. I wouldn't dare let my husband hear me pray those prayers! Yet, I knew that new place of employment was the right place for me to be at such a time in my life.

Though I "knew" all this was in God's plan, it seemed I wanted to hear other people's opinion. I talked with a few people who I thought would give me a few words of encouragement about my decision to accept the job so far away. However, it seemed the only thing I got was negative feedback. I heard many comments from many different people even though I didn't even ask all of them for their opinions. Some frivolous comments were such as the following: What are you going to do when you get married? What are you going to do when you get pregnant? How much is it going to cost for gas and car repair? What if your car breaks down? Isn't it silly for you to even consider the drive? Do you have a hole in your head to drive 64 miles one way from home to work every day? Won't that commute be boring? The pay is not worth it, is it? And the list goes on! Well, many simple decisions are usually hard for me to make, such as where will I go to eat lunch, what will I order for lunch, what color outfit do I want, etc. I considered accepting the job out of town to be a major decision for me; so, when I made such a major decision to commute so far away, I felt confident that I had made the right job decision. I KNOW that it was the leading of the Holy Spirit.

Even after I accepted the job, others constantly criticized me for making such a terrible decision. Some people sneered when they found out my starting salary and said it was crazy for me to drive that far for X amount of money and that they would never do that. But, I felt such a peace within and knew I had made the right decision. I can say this for sure—you had better be sure it is God who tells you what to do and when the time is right to do it! If not, people will have you constantly going in circles. (This is a warning to someone reading this book right now so take heed!)

I kept asking the Lord about my purpose for working out of town but He never told me enough (I thought) until years later. I left home many days in tears during the extreme heat, during the heavy downpour, and during the snow. I would ask the Lord how long was I to continue my commute under such conditions that far away from home. The strange thing about this whole matter is that I loved my job and I loved the people with whom I worked. I am not saying that there were not challenging days, of course, there were some. I was tested many days on my job but with each test I wanted to show Jesus in me and do the right thing by being humble and obedient. Through all of this, GOD HAD A PLAN!

God allowed my employment out of town to serve as a training camp for my ministry. First of all, I believe the long commute prepared me for itinerant ministry because I knew I would travel spreading the Good News. Therefore, I had to be faithful to my secular boss in this endeavor. This commute disciplined me to be ready to go anywhere, at any time, and most of all, to be ON TIME. Secondly, it seems, God allowed me to work directly for one of the toughest but most respected men at that public utility company, Mr. Bill McCall, Jr. When I first started working for him, I appeared rather timid and shy, some thought. The reason I said, THOUGHT, was because many times I had things on my tongue to say but the Lord would not allow me to speak (that's right). Therefore, others thought I was afraid or too intimidated to say what I needed to say. But as time went on, I found myself speaking openly and frankly about issues that needed to be addressed.

Because so many employees knew Mr. McCall, and knew of his high expectations, I had very little difficulty establishing relationships and working with other departments within the company. I simply told them that my boss needs such and such paperwork by a specified time and sure enough, I would get immediate attention. I, personally, wanted to know what was it about this man that caused people to respond to his requests and react the way they did in his presence. And trust me, God allowed me various opportunities to find this out first hand. Well, because I worked directly with him, God allowed me to focus on things that I would need as a part of my ministry training.

In the natural, the first thing I discovered was my ability to use Mr. McCall's name and get immediate results. Spiritually, I was being trained to believe the more in Jesus and trust Him that He will do what the Word declares He will do in John 14:13-14, "And whatsoever ye shall ask in my name, that will I do, that the Father may be glorified in the Son. If ye shall ask anything in my name, I will do it." And the Word goes on to tell us about using the name of Jesus in various other scriptures. I further discovered and acknowledged that in the natural Mr. McCall exhibited characteristics of which I was supposed to take note of. Some things about him that I admired and perceived to be of spiritual benefit included his ability to exercise good judgment, not easily intimidated, possessed wisdom, highly respected, very persuasive, firm, intelligent, high work standards, very detailed, very challenging, super memory, hard and dedicated worker, humorous, and handled criticism professionally. Sounds like qualities any preacher would like to possess—including me!!

One might argue that I only discovered "positive" traits or characteristics about my boss, knowing that we all have some weaknesses or faults. Well, God is a good God and He knows what He is preparing me for in ministry. God wanted me to concentrate on the good so that I may learn to be an ambassador for Him during my training. Believe me, I had enough weaknesses or faults of my own and God wanted to improve those areas of weaknesses in order to make me more functional, and thus, more effective for His kingdom. Isn't that what training is all about? I needed to see firsthand the benefits of possessing these qualities.

After I received my necessary training as God had predestined, Mr. McCall was promoted and I was no longer under his immediate supervision. But guess what? I noticed that I must have learned something special from him because I noticed how people would listen, react and respond to me as I made my reports or requested information from them. As a matter of fact, many employees told me that they could tell Mr. McCall had trained me because I am detailed just like he is. So I concluded that I must have learned what I was predestined to learn from him because many people saw some of him in me. In biblical times, that is what the people were saying about Peter and John after they had been around Jesus for a while. If you don't believe me read Acts 4:13, "Now when they saw the boldness of Peter and John, and perceived that they were unlearned and ignorant men, they marveled; and they took knowledge of them, that they had been with Jesus."

As you might have concluded, some of Jesus' persona was seen in His followers. This is exactly what we are to expect when we spend time with Jesus and witness for Him. We should want people to see Jesus in us. We are to want people to listen, to react to what they have heard from us, and to make a change through our witness as the Holy Spirit directs us. Yes, God was grooming me for my ministry so that when the time came, I would be ready. It is hard to appreciate discipline while you are being trained. Blatantly, I believe life itself generates situations in which you can apply what you have learned and at the same time you reap benefits from your training. My experience attest to the fact that teachers usually test students on materials covered in class; so, don't think you are just being trained spiritually so that you can escape life without a test.

As a matter of fact, I believe in my heart that just prior to my departure from employment [through early retirement], my training was being tested. I believe that God allowed the very man whom I had emulated during my training (employment, I mean) to be instrumental in my testing. I had to obey God in the midst of opposition and do something publicly that had never been done before in the history of my employment. God allowed a situation to develop in which Mr. McCall desperately needed to hear a word from the Lord. Amazingly, I was in the midst of it out of compassion and a sincere desire to be a blessing to God's children. I stood boldly and faced fear, opposition, criticism, and even pride. But at the same time, I had to accomplish my mission or fulfill my assignment of conducting a prayer service on behalf of one of the key men at this public utility company, my trainer. I had been tested in the same areas of which I had earlier completed ministry training. I can't tell you when the boldness came into my life but I know it was there on time.

You probably won't believe this, but evidently, Satan was outraged with me for obeying and glorifying God through that prayer service at work. It was only a few weeks after the prayer service at work that the spirit of witchcraft was sent to attack my family and me through a so-called prayer service. Yet, the God we serve is so faithful and will not leave us hanging on a limb when we follow His order.

During that same prayer service at work, God revealed so much to me in such a short period of time. Something I can share from the experience is that not everyone who you expect to support you will stand with you when you really need him or her to support you the most. I found out that people would make the most ridiculous excuses for their absence when they find out that things went successfully—even without their support. I found out that God would sometimes use the most unlikely person to bless us during our trials. I found out that some people don't want any part of a public religious ceremony. Call me a religious fanatic if you wish, but I will tell you this—when you love the Lord and want to obey Him, you will find yourself doing some very unusual things for Him. You must be willing to carry out your mission no matter where you are, no matter what it takes, or no matter who is <u>not</u> there to support you. If you are willing to obey, God will prepare the way for you to accomplish your mission.

Try to remember all of your discipline as you go through different trials because as a teacher might say "You WILL see this again on your exam!" Sometimes it pays to watch where God sends us and to take note of the people He sends our way. If you don't get an immediate revelation, just keep paying attention to your surroundings, keep praying, and you will be surprised what God will <u>show</u> you, even if He doesn't <u>tell</u> you at the time.

To this very day, I am so glad that I obeyed the voice of the Lord and accepted the accounting job out of town. Moreover, I am glad that I was available and prepared to be instrumental in physical and spiritual healing for Mr. McCall. Yes, the very man whom God predestined to hire me and train me on the job was the very man who God allowed me to bless through my spiritual preparation. It seems conducting this prayer service on the job was my final exam while employed. I suffered pain at the hand of Satan for being an instrument for God; but if I had to do it all over again, I WOULD.

Now I am no longer employed due to my early retirement. However, I do believe that God publicly rewarded me with an early retirement for my obedience to Him during my training and for having the prayer service at my job to bless the man of God. Even after I retired, Mr. McCall and I have crossed paths on numerous occasions as he shares the blessings of God through his powerful testimony.

Chapter Five
God Changed Rules To Fulfill A Prophecy

God Changed Rules
To Fulfill A Prophecy

Let me tell you something, Satan doesn't know all of God's plans. Satan was out to kill, steal, and destroy my family and me. During the last few weeks of my employment, I was in so much pain; I don't know how I endured the agony and pain. Yet, the <u>timing</u> of my retirement in relation to the satanic attack of witchcraft had to be orchestrated by God. When that spirit of witchcraft was sent to destroy me, God had already prepared me through a vision about my early retirement. Paperwork was in process and all I had to do was inform my boss of my decision. I know Satan didn't know all of this.

This is the revelation about my early retirement: Here it was the Fourth of July 1999 and I was sitting on my bed crying because I was too tired to participate in any activities with my children. So already feeling a little depressed, I kept thinking about the time I spent away from my children in order to work. It seems I wanted to quit work, stay home, and take care of my children; but I knew that I could not afford to quit work. I thought about the many days I left home and would start crying as soon as I backed out the garage because I didn't want to leave my children to go to work. Anyhow, later during this beautiful Fourth of July evening, something changed in the atmosphere and my pity party was over.

This very same day, July 4, 1999, God gave me a word about my situation. The Holy Spirit revealed to me that I would be financially secure enough to retire from my job and be home with the boys by the time I was 45 years old. Well, I recorded what the Holy Spirit revealed to me but I had all kinds of reasons to doubt this was the Holy Spirit revealing this fact to me. First of all, I was already 42 years old at the time of this revelation and could not foresee us acquiring the amount of money needed for my retirement. Secondly, according to the retirement rules, I had to be 55 years old and have 25 years of service or I had to have 30 years of service—I had neither. Thirdly, if I wanted to buy some years to make me eligible later, it would have cost me over $100,000 to do so—I didn't have that money either.

While I was making plans for retirement and waiting to see God move on my behalf, the enemy was making plans to get me fired. The enemy tried to use witchcraft on my family and me, which if God didn't have a plan in place, I, possibly, could have been <u>fired</u> from my job and missed my early retirement. Just prior to my retirement, I recall getting phone calls about every Tuesday reporting that one or both of my boys were sick. Some days I would ask for my child to please remain at school until dismissal, just to keep from taking off work and giving in to the enemy's attack. I recall checking on the boys' progress in school, and each time, I received unfavorable responses that their grades were falling. There were times I wanted so desperately to explain my situation to the boys' teachers; but at the same time I did not want the teachers to think that I was seeking sympathy or favoritism.

My husband and my boys are very dear to me and the enemy attacked my children in an attempt to defeat me and to keep my mind off the things of God. (The more I think about it, I believe witchcraft was involved when my husband experienced his bout with cancer). Anyhow, both of my boys were experiencing sickness or injuries. It seemed I experienced the most problems with my youngest son, Nicholas. He would often tell me that it felt like someone had a rope tied around his head. I could not tell my son that Mommy was feeling the same way he felt. I tried not to make a big deal out of his complaint in an effort to try and console him. There were times I would punish him for his inconsistent behavior in school and his lack of concentration on his schoolwork. Yet, I would then turn around and feel very guilty because I knew the source of his mind wandering episodes, etc. But, still, it seemed no one would ever understand our extent of suffering. It was so hard to see my child with a constant headache or a constant spell of vomiting for no apparent reason. I recall when we went on vacation for the first time during this witchcraft episode, Nicholas got extremely sick for no apparent reason. I asked Russell to take Justin along with him and for them to try to have fun. I spent my entire vacation time in the hotel ministering to Nicholas, praying that he would feel well and cleaning up his vomit. I believe Nicholas detected and felt my hurt as well because I recall him telling me "Mommy, everything will be alright." I recall the time when Justin had a cast on his leg and Nicholas had a cast on his arm during the same period. Oh, God, I was so mad with the enemy for attacking my innocent children with witchcraft. Seeing my children suffer was much more difficult than bearing my own pain. Despite all of the sickness, God had a plan and He is always ahead of the enemy's plan. The enemy didn't know that God was setting me up for a permanent blessing, my early retirement. You see—I didn't know back in 1999 that Satan would attack my children and me with witchcraft just prior to my 45th birthday, but God knew all about it.

Through all of the sicknesses, etc., I still planned for my retirement because Habakkuk 2:3 reminded me "For the vision is yet for an appointed time, but at the end it shall speak, and not lie: though it tarry, wait for it; because it will surely come, it will not tarry." So, I said, "Lord, I heard what you said but I just don't see how you are going to make that happen. I don't have the age or the money to make this retirement prophecy come to pass but I know you told me it would happen."

Though I kept questioning God, I remained confident that it was the Holy Spirit who revealed this secret of my early retirement to me. The words to me were so plain and powerful; I knew it was from God. I gained confidence and told my husband what the Holy Spirit had revealed to me; but Russell only laughed at me. In addition, I told the story to one of my friends and I even told her that I don't see anyway possible for this to happen, but God said it to me. So, as time went on I kept confessing the prophecy to myself and I would write little notes to myself such as "I will retire in 2 years" (or whatever the timeframe was when I was writing).

One day a friend came to my office and asked about my plans to retire since I had only one year left based on what I had said a few years ago. I couldn't say very much because I didn't have a lot of information, but I still believed God. My friend didn't know it, but those words in the form of a question were like a test from God for me to confirm whether or not I was going to continue to believe the prophecy or not. Well, I would often read a scripture and/or listen to other people talk about their faith. The Lord let me know that the word or revelation that He gives me will not profit me if I don't mix the word with faith and have patience. I recalled overhearing someone say one day that we should fear God and that God is not a man that He should lie. And sure enough I kept reading scriptures that encouraged me to believe what God had revealed unto me. Psalm 115:13-14 say: "He will bless them that fear the Lord, both small and great. The Lord shall increase you more and more, you and your children." Psalm 118:8 affirms: "It is better to trust in God than to put confidence in man."

There were just so many scriptures that helped build my faith in the promise that God gave me about my early retirement. GUESS WHAT? God allowed the retirement rules to change, which now made me eligible to retire with only 28 years of service, instead of 30 years, and no age restriction. The changes also lowered the percentage of money required to purchase retirement time from 52% to 35%. I said, Lord, the people who approved those retirement changes do not know me, but you allowed them to change those retirement rules to fulfill a prophecy to ME. When those rules changed, it seemed things shifted in the spirit realm for me.

Remember the words of the school district bookkeeper that begged me to leave my retirement funds alone? She told me that I would be glad later if I listened to her—well, bless the Lord, her words came to pass and helped fulfill my answer to prayer. By the time I turned 45 years old, I had 25 years of service on the retirement system record and required the purchase of only three additional years of service at the reduced rate to qualify for full retirement benefits. I got busy praying some more and making plans IN MY MIND because the next step was for me to FIND enough money to purchase the three years of service time. Of course, I DID NOT have the money and did not see how I would get the money, even though the amount was substantially lower after the retirement changes. I said, okay, Lord, I need $60,000 in order for me to retire, not $100,000.

How was I going to pay this money and not cause any hardship to my family? GUESS WHAT? God started giving me strategies that were almost unbelievable and I knew God had his hand on my life and my pocketbook. I never stopped paying my tithe and I never neglected my family in anyway financially. Yes, it took lots of fasting, praying, and believing and listening to God. Somehow, through God's strategies, I saved just above the amount required in the exact specified time that I needed. I gave my letter of intent to retire to my boss the same month I turned 45 years old. Everyone was shocked! I even pinched myself just to be sure I was still alert and was not dreaming. On my very last day of employment, my co-workers gave me a beautiful retirement luncheon and parting gifts, all of which I will treasure.

My husband made plans to rent a facility and extend the retirement celebration by inviting our children and other friends and relatives as a personal tribute. However, I begged him to cancel his plans because there were still some issues about my pains, etc. and he respected my request.

It is not significant that I retired at 45 years of age. What is significant is that the Holy Spirit gave me the revelation over three years in advance, when I was only 42. Furthermore, I had already revealed the matter to a devoted friend. My God remained faithful to His Word even though rules had to be changed to make it transpire. By the way, I called that bookkeeper that is also now retired, and thanked her for allowing God to use her to tell me to leave my retirement funds alone. She was greatly honored to receive my telephone call. *Let others know. Thank them for their obedience.*

I thought I was just going to sit back and relax with my children that first year of retirement; but instead, it was spent mostly fighting in spiritual warfare against Satan who was using church people to try to destroy my family and me. No one will ever be able to understand the degree of pain and emotional distress that I experienced during this warfare. As a matter of fact, I kept smiling but every now and then someone told me that I looked tired and worn out. This tired and worn out look was captured and evidenced in some of my retirement snap shots.

I finally made it to retirement! I did retire early just as God revealed it to me and this special time allows me to spend more time with the boys at school as well as in my prayer closet. Satan cannot prevail because God's favor is still upon my family and I bless Him through all of our struggles. Oh, God is so faithful. Lamentations 3:23 say: "…great is thy faithfulness." So, if the Holy Spirit reveals something to you, just trust Him and give Him time. That's the God I serve and I will ever love and trust Him. When God

I HAD TO DIE EXPOSING WITCHCRAFT IN THE CHURCH

tells you something, it's better than money in the bank. I will tell you again: GOD IS FAITHFUL. Yes, that's my Father! He keeps on blessing me over and over again!

Chapter Six
My Encounter With Witchcraft
And
False Prophecy

My Encounter With Witchcraft And False Prophecy

The prologue to my testimony may be an extensive one, but consider, my story is not hearsay. I am telling you what I personally experienced. My intent is to expose witchcraft in the church and manifest the power of God by sharing some experiences along with various scripture references. All acclamations to Jesus!

Witchcraft and false prophecy are two activities that Satan uses to deceive and control people; yet, many people cannot discern these demonic activities in the church. According to Hosea 4:6, "My people are destroyed for lack of knowledge: because thou hast rejected knowledge, I will also reject thee…."

When I discuss witchcraft, some people might immediately think that I am ignorant or am just using the term as a crutch for my own weakness. I have heard people describe Christians that way also. Such thoughts are far from the truth. There are many questions that I could ask you right now to find out how much you know about witchcraft and false prophecy. Do you have anyone or do you know of anyone who has a sickness of which the symptoms are hard to explain to a friend or even to a doctor? Do you ever wonder why there are people who would congregate to conspire to harm or control other people for no apparent reason? Do you know that witchcraft can affect an entire community? Read Daniel 10:13 where it tells us how Daniel's prayer was hindered. Do you find it strange that some small communities only have three or four funerals a year while there may be one community of the same size with nearly twenty funerals in a year? Do you know that there are people who worship Satan and request supernatural powers from Satan to send demonic spirits your way just to torment, control, or even destroy you because they cannot have power over you in the natural realm? Have you ever heard of witchcraft? Open your eyes and open your ears that you might hear the truth! Are you hungry for the truth? Well, Galatians 5:19-23, (emphasis added) reads: "Now the works of the flesh are manifest, which are these: Adultery, fornication, uncleanness, lasciviousness, Idolatry, **WITCHCRAFT**, hatred, variance, emulations, wrath, strife, seditions, heresies, envyings, murders, drunkenness, revellings, and such like: of the which I tell you before, as I have also told you in time past, that they which do such things shall not inherit the kingdom of God." Just pause and think for a second: do you agree that if adultery still exists, then so does witchcraft, since it is also a work of the flesh? Do you know that there is a counterfeit to the Holy Spirit? Do you know that there is such thing as a 'religious' spirit?

I preached a sermon one Sunday entitled "Copy Cat." The sermon informed the congregation that Satan could present himself to us like he is God. Satan has people strategically planted to oppose the things of God. These people can act spiritual by shouting, speaking in tongues, healing the sick (surely Satan can take sickness away since he gave it to you), prophesying, etc. According to Matthew 7:23, "Not everyone that saith unto me, Lord, Lord, shall enter into the kingdom of heaven; but he that doeth the will of my Father which is in heaven. Many will say to me in that day, Lord, Lord, have we not prophesied in thy name? And in thy name have cast out devils? And in thy name done many wonderful works? And then will I profess unto them, I never knew you: depart from me, ye that work iniquity." These people want the anointing that God's people possess but they don't want to fast, pray, seek God's face and wait for power from God.

Instead, these people summon power from Satan to do the work or put on the show for them to manifest to the public. The perpetrator normally does all the dirty work behind the scene. Therefore, the perpetrator can go undetected for a long time. They try to be 'copy cats' of God's anointed people and thus deceive many people. Evidently, witchcraft is real for the Bible speaks of it. Acts 8:9-11 reveal, "But there was a certain man, called Simon, which beforetime in the same city used sorcery, and bewitched the people of Samaria, giving out that himself was some great one: To whom they all gave heed from the least to the greatest, saying, This man is the great power of God. And to him they had regard, because that of a long time he had bewitched them with sorceries." This one man had deceived and controlled a number of people through WITCHCRAFT for a long time.

Also, Acts 13:6 declares, "And when they had gone through the isle unto Pa-phos, they found a certain sorcerer, a false prophet, a Jew, whose name was Bar-je-sus." Please read these stories and find out what happened to these sorcerers.

If that is not enough to convince you, then flip back to the Old Testament and read Exodus 7:11 "Then Pharaoh also called the wise men and the sorcerers: now the magicians of Egypt, they also did in like manner with their enchantments." So from this, you can see that witchcraft has been around for a long time. This is nothing new—people just don't preach about it like they use to!!

Many people do not believe in demonic forces and hence do not believe in the power of God to fight and overcome demonic forces. Whether people believe this truth or not, witchcraft and false prophecy are still in full operation in our churches today. Some may ask for more information about witchcraft. Well, let's go to the Bible again BEFORE I share my face-to-face experience.

First, let's go to Revelation 2:20 which reads, "…Thou sufferest that woman Jezebel, which calleth herself a prophetess, to teach and to seduce my servants…" Sure, she called herself a prophetess, but what did she do? Let's go to II Kings 9:22 (emphasis added), "…What peace, so long as the whoredoms of thy mother Jezebel and her **WITCHCRAFTS** are so many?" Again, what did she do? Well, it is going to take you some time to answer that question (Come on, get your Bible and read the scriptures).

1) Jezebel disliked God's true prophets (I Kings 18:13)

2) Jezebel used her own little group to do her dirty work (I Kings 19:2)

3) She used tactics of fear and intimidation (I Kings 19:2-3)

4) She used manipulation, praise, control, and false witnesses (I Kings 21:7-11)

5) She encouraged her husband to do evil before God (I Kings 21:25)

6) She wanted to be the center of attention (II Kings 9:30)

7) She <u>finally</u> got the punishment she deserved (II Kings 9:33-37)

Now, once upon a time my grandfather told me about Jezebel. But, he only told me that people who wear makeup look like Jezebel (oh, oh, I'm guilty). I read and found out that Jezebel did wear makeup (I Kings 9:30). But, after I had a personal encounter with a false prophetess, I decided to search the scriptures for myself. I found out that the very things that Jezebel did back then are still active among people today and that her influence was more in-depth and involved more grave frivolities than merely wearing makeup. Jezebel was a threatening force to God's people THEN and her demonic spirit still threatens the body of Christ TODAY. (Read about my prayer meeting experience further in the text to query items 1-7 above for a paradigm).

In my opinion, witchcraft infiltrates the victim's mind and is a satanic work that leaves very little evidence that leads to the perpetrator. However, through God's revelation, all of Satan's tactics can be revealed. I know this is true because I experienced a spiritual confrontation with witchcraft and God revealed much of the scheme to me. Yet, many people looked at me as if I were the devil when I would say to them that witchcraft is real and is prevalent among church workers.

My intent is to expose the works of Satan and at the same time show you the power of God over the spirit of witchcraft. Yes, many people's eyes are so blinded; they refuse to believe the truth. As a matter of fact, I was told by a number of people not to say anything about my experience that I am about to share with you!! Some people wanted me to withhold this powerful testimony from the public.

What if David did not tell about his enemies and all the evil that King Saul had done unto him? And what if the disciples did not write about their experiences, about their arguments, and about other people who tried to do them harm? What if Jesus didn't tell us in the Bible that Peter denied Him? What if Jesus had concealed the fact that He told Satan, who was using Peter, to get behind Him? Throughout Second Timothy, Chapter Four, Paul revealed to Timothy some of the people, by name, that had done him evil so that Timothy would also be aware of Satan's workers. According to Second Timothy 4:14, Paul even told how Alexander, the coppersmith, had done "much evil" unto him but God had shown vengeance and paid Alexander for his evil.

We Christians should also share some of our experiences to make others aware of whom to avoid when we, in fact, know where evil exists. Pastors are to be careful whom they invite to "pray" over the congregation. Laypersons are to be careful whom they allow to lay hands and pray over them. I am not saying any of this is wrong (I also perform this rite as the Lord leads me), I am only saying <u>be careful</u>. We are to try the spirits, but the individual who is trying the spirit must have the Holy Spirit in order to adequately identify the opposite spirit. Based on this rationale, I share my experience so that someone else will know that witchcraft is real. But do not be perplexed or dismayed, we have a risen Savior who defeated Satan when He went to the cross, went down in the grave, and got back up, and is alive forever more! Hallelujah!!

    I found out that God would often use the gift of prophecy to warn and prepare me for danger ahead, to encourage me during adversity, and even to give me direction. However, God not only speaks through prophecy, God is God and He can bless us and warn us any way He chooses. I found out that many of MY blessings of encouragement came through the word of true prophecies. Second Chronicles 20:20 tells us "…Believe in the Lord your God, so shall ye be established; believe his prophets, so shall ye prosper." Now, remember, when prophecies are given, you have to do what is necessary to bring the prophecies to pass. For example, if the prophecy says that you will get a job at a specific place; then you should at least go and fill out the job application if you had not already done so (Get the point?). And I must warn you that you can't tell everybody what God speaks to YOU through prophecy because some people will get jealous and possibly try to hinder your blessings. Remember what happened to Joseph in the book of Genesis? His very own brothers were angry with him because of his dreams and tried to destroy him.

    I have had several ministers to prophesy to me on numerous occasions. For the most part, I have many of the prophecies recorded. I thank God that I recorded them because they serve as reminders to me of what God has in store for me. I review my recorded prophecies periodically and I have noticed that different people, who I have only met once in my life, have prophesied to me the most. The true prophecies are always consistent with God's Word. Furthermore, prophecy should be used to build up people, not tear them down or 'beat them down'. So, from time to time, as God has instructed me to do, I also review the prophetic words to see which of them have already come to fruition. The Word tells me in Deuteronomy 18:22 that "When a prophet speaketh in the name of the Lord, if the thing follow not, nor come to pass, that is the thing which the Lord hath not spoken, but the prophet hath spoken it presumptuously...." Thank God many of the prophecies to me have come to pass and I am waiting for God's timing for some others to come to pass. Many of the prophecies that I received are confirmation to things the Holy Spirit had already revealed to me in prayer.

The Holy Spirit Himself has revealed future events to me about my early retirement, my ministry, this first book, etc. Nevertheless, I think the most profound and timely prophecy that I have ever received came to me one Sunday evening from **Prophet David Barr** of Abundant Harvest Church in Georgetown, South Carolina. First of all, I did not make plans to attend his church this day. As a matter of fact, I was already at another church enjoying some gospel singing when the Holy Spirit prompted me to leave and attend Prophet Barr's service.

When I arrived at Abundant Harvest Church, I found out that service was about to close for the night. Anyhow, obeying the Holy Spirit, I pulled my hat down a little bit to cover my face, entered the sanctuary, and sat on the very last seat in the church as not to cause any further disruption. Then I whispered under my breath and said, "Lord why would you tell me to leave a church where I was enjoying the singing and send me to a church where the service has ended?" I didn't hear a response from the Holy Spirit so then I said, "Lord, I am so sorry that I lied on you. I really thought you told me to leave that other service and come to this church."

NOW LOOK AT GOD WORK: as Prophet Barr was standing in front of the altar to give the benediction, he told the congregation that he could not close the service yet. Then he looked to the back of the church and said, "I want the young lady at the back of the church with the hat on to come up here." Naturally, I lifted my hat a little bit and looked around to see if there was anyone else on the back seat that had on a hat other than myself. In that instance, I realized that it had to be ME; he had called ME up front. When I walked up front, he just looked at me and there was total silence in the sanctuary while he looked at me. By this time, I was nervous, my knees were knocking and I knew for certain that it was God who had directed me to this church tonight. As I stood there, my heart was pounding and inwardly I was saying, "Lord, what is it this time?" Prophet Barr began his utterance under the unction of the Holy Spirit and his prophecy included these words to me:

> "This is a word from the Lord. This is your time of deliverance. What you have already endured, no one will believe it. Sometimes you wanted to know how did you overcome. The enemy wanted to force you into a nervous breakdown. You are a woman after God's own heart. You try to beat yourself down for what God

has already forgiven you for. You will have to crucify this flesh even more. You lust to do the things that please God, but in a fleshly way. You have to wait for God's timing. Things will work out so that you can just turn the key. You don't have to break down anything to get what you need. You won't have to break the key off to try to get whatever you touch. God has given you the wisdom to overcome/ handle whatever comes your way. You have been doing what God has required of you. You were at the end of your rope so to speak and wanted to find a way out of what you were going through. You are hurt and no one knows."

These are all of the key words that I have recorded about this prophecy and the sentences may not necessarily be in the order of which they were spoken to me. Nevertheless, I left the front of the church that night with my face wet with tears because I knew the various times that I had been hurt in life and no one really knew about it. But my deeper tears came when I saw the faithfulness of God by directing me to a place for comfort and future guidance and protection.

That prophecy may seem like a lot of mixed up sentences and fragments with no special meaning to many people; however, I believe the Holy Spirit allowed me to capture and record every word that would play a significant part in my life that night and in the future. Moreover, with the Holy Spirit's interpretation, EVERY word will have some significance and give a special direction for MY life simply because it was specifically for me. When I first heard some of those prophetic words, I MUST ADMIT, I was about to doubt the prophecy because I knew I had never experienced a nervous breakdown in my entire life. BUT, these words were enough to cause me to seek God for clarification and direction. Sure enough, the Lord later revealed to me that this prophecy is true but is to sustain me during a future event in my life, even though the prophet used past tense. (Usage of the past tense is what caused my doubt). Those few sentences gave me a word of prophecy and assurance because the prophet said "This is a word from the Lord" (I did overcome); he gave me a word of knowledge when he said "The enemy wanted to force you into a nervous breakdown"; and he gave a word of wisdom when he said "God will show you how to handle whatever comes your way."

That prophecy from God through Prophet Barr prepared me for one of the greatest battles in my life thus far and I know that it was given by God to encourage and strengthen me along the way. Even though the prophecy revealed the beginning and ending of the battle, lots of pain took place in the middle. I HAD TO DO MY PART! I had to fast, pray, believe, and yes, I had to WAIT! And by the way, I did not have to pay Prophet Barr to receive that prophecy from the Lord. As a matter of fact, I forgot and did not even leave a penny for offering at the church that night. Needless to say, I have often given love gifts to ministers and do not mind giving love offerings. I clarified I did not have to pay for a prophecy because I know there are ministries out there that will tell you to send them a certain amount of money and they will tell you what the Lord says. Romans 15:27 admonishes us to bless ministers "For if the Gentiles have been made partakers of their spiritual things, their duty is also to minister unto them in carnal things." I do NOT have to pay money or render any other services for any true prophet to give me a word from the Lord. God's prophets (I did say God's prophets) are all special gifts to us from God as part of the body of Christ. It is fine to give offerings, but please know that you do not have to pay money to hear from God. God knows when we, His children, need to hear a fresh word from Him. Proverbs 15:23 declares, "...and a word spoken in due season, how good is it!" That shows you how good God is. He knows what we need and when we need it.

Yes, every now and then we need to hear a fresh word from the Lord. A word of caution: Not everyone you see coming has "Jesus on his/her mind." Please be aware that just as there are prophets and other people out there to bless you, Satan has someone out there to try to curse you. As a matter of fact, Ba'lak tried to hire Ba'-laam to curse the Israelites. Let us look at Numbers 22:6-17: "Come now therefore, I pray thee, curse me this people; for they are too mighty for me: peradventure I shall prevail, that we may smite them, and that I may drive them out of the land: for I wot that he whom thou blessest is blessed, and he whom thou cursest is cursed...For I will promote thee unto very great honour, and I will do whatsoever thou sayest unto me: come therefore, I pray thee, curse me this people." Then Deuteronomy 23:4-5 declares, "...They hired against thee Ba'laam ... to curse thee. Nevertheless the Lord thy God would not hearken unto Ba'laam; but the Lord thy God turned the curse into a blessing unto thee, because the Lord thy God loved thee." God loves His people and will send godly people in your life to bless you but Satan is out to destroy us at any cost.

In Matthew 7:15, Jesus warns us of false prophets and declares, "Beware of false prophets, which come to you in sheep's clothing, but inwardly they are ravening wolves." I want you to know that God's Word must come to pass. Jeremiah 29:8-9 declare, "For thus saith the Lord of hosts, the God of Israel; let not your prophets and your diviners, that be in the midst of you, deceive you, neither hearken to your dreams which ye cause to be dreamed. For they prophesy falsely unto you in my name: I have not sent them, saith the Lord." In First Timothy 4:1, the scripture says, "Now the Spirit speaketh expressly, that in the latter times some shall depart from the faith, giving heed to seducing spirits, and doctrines of devils;" Also, Matthew 24:11 states, "And many false prophets shall rise, and shall deceive many." But I want you to know that God will take care of the false prophets. I encourage you to read Jeremiah, Chapter 24; Deuteronomy 13:1-6; Deuteronomy, Chapter 18; and other passages to witness some of the actions and the punishment that God gave to the false prophets.

Yes, indeed, I have already had my experience with this warning that came directly from Jesus Himself in Matthew 24:11 which declares, "And many false prophets shall rise, and shall deceive many." One morning on my way to work, the Holy Spirit said to me, "In time of peace, prepare for war." I really did not understand what the Spirit was saying to me. Yet, I wrote the words down while I was driving and later stuck the note on the wall in my office. Two weeks after the prophecy by Prophet Barr and only days after this warning about 'war', the enemy attacked. I had a face-to-face encounter with a false prophetess who would have destroyed my life if

I HAD TO DIE EXPOSING WITCHCRAFT IN THE CHURCH

I didn't cling to the Word of God. (Remember my earlier discussion about Jezebel and witchcraft? Now compare that to my experience).

I was invited to attend a prayer meeting at a church where a prophetess from out of town would be ministering. It didn't occur to me at the time, that this particular prayer service was being held on a Tuesday night instead of the regularly scheduled Wednesday night prayer services. Anyhow, the Holy Spirit directed me to attend and take along with me the pad that contained all of my previously recorded prophecies.

When I entered the meeting room, I was a little uncomfortable but nonetheless full of anticipation for the night's agenda. There were about twelve people in attendance. Seven of the attendees were referred to as "seven praying women." There was also a church leader and the spouse, the prophetess and her partner, and myself. For some strange reasons, as I looked upon different ones faces they were shocked to see me present. As a matter of fact, the person who invited me had to apologize to that leader for inviting me. I immediately sensed that things were not conducive for a prayer meeting atmosphere.

During the initial discussion, I observed how the visiting prophetess was writing down some things in her notebook as the attendees were telling her about their situation (and they were even telling her about personal matters pertaining to their absent family members). During their discussion, the prophetess mentioned that there were some members on that church's roll who needed to be removed from the church, etc. She then proceeded to ask the other attendees whether they had prayed at 5 a.m., 12 O'clock noon, and 6 p.m. as she previously instructed. The prophetess then warned them that they all needed to be sure to pray at those appointed times. She also told them (us) that we have to locate our enemies.

The first thing I recall that she said directly to me was "You're very quiet tonight." I replied that I am normally quiet in a setting like the one we were in and that I just wanted to learn. She then asked me what problems I was having (as she had already asked some others). As the Holy Spirit directed me, I told her that I didn't have any problems that I haven't already prayed about (smiling). Oh my, when I said that, the rest of the meeting was spent attacking ME. She then said to me, "You have a self-righteous spirit—trying to make people think you are so much more than you are." She told me that my smile is not real and there is much more behind my smile than people know. When I heard those comments and saw how the others were looking as if in agreement with her, I was bewildered because I knew the truth was not spoken about me. But then I thought—it is only pride that won't let you admit this truth that she is telling you about yourself. This strange woman continued to say all kinds of negative things to me in front of everyone at the meeting and they all appeared to be impressed with the prophetess. Thank God I knew that true prophecies are to build up and comfort, not tear down and destroy. Heartbreakingly, the prophetess continued and told me that there is a lot of stuff in me that needs to come out. Yes, finally, there is some truth mixed among a lot of lies. I admit that I had to die from a lot of 'stuff' in my life—and I am still dying from this flesh. I even recall the prophecy from Prophet Barr that warns: I will have to crucify this flesh even more. He also said that I try to please God in a fleshly way. So, yes, the prophetess was right about that part. Let's remember, though, that Satan had some truth mixed with his lies when he spoke to Eve against God in the book of Genesis. The prophetess told me that I was not ready to pray for anyone else until I get myself straightened out. Suddenly, the church leader interjected and said that I was 'deceitful too'. Feeling entrapped, all of a sudden, I acquired boldness and asked that leader if he was "praying for me or against me." After this saying, the prophetess became irate with me and said that she was going to show everybody who I really was that night.

She continuously slandered me and asked me personal questions about my economic status, type lifestyle I live, the ages of my children, and whether my children were saved and had received the Holy Ghost with speaking in tongues. She further asked me if I was saved, had the Holy Ghost, and spoke in tongues. Trying to treat the leader's guest with respect, I tried to answer her questions with vague responses, instead of remaining silent. Through all of this torture, one thing she said stayed on my mind constantly. She said as long as you have children you will have something to pray for! (Let me interject one thing here. After this meeting, my children were either sick or getting hurt every Tuesday thereafter for months. Their grades were plummeting and even I, myself, had excruciating 'sticking' head pains every day and night for months that were so intense, I will not be able to fully describe them even if I tried. Remember Prophet Barr said, "What you have already endured, no one will believe it." I knew all this was a satanic attack that originated as a result of that "prayer meeting." When I realized what was happening, I fasted and prayed the same hours that the prophetess had the group to pray as to counter attack their curse. God later broke that curse from my children and me. (I will address this more in depth later).

Now, back to the meeting. As I sat and observed the way I was slandered, I tried to take notes about what was going on but the prophetess strongly and harshly demanded that I put my pencil down. My hand began to tremble and my writing became illegible for a period. I don't know whether I was that nervous as a result of trying to record as much as possible or whether some demonic force was activated. As I tried to finish one more word, the prophetess harshly spoke to me saying, "I said put that pencil down now!" As you can see, the spirit of control was very much in operation. I was not allowed to use my own paper and pencil that I brought to the church. *Where the spirit is, there is liberty*

She continued to tell me that I am going to have to learn to listen to somebody and that I don't know everything. She said I am going to have to learn to follow instructions because she didn't tell anyone to write down anything. I was also asked why was I in attendance anyway and what was I expecting by being present at the meeting. It was about this time that the leader told me that if I tell what happened at the prayer service that night, he would roll me down the aisle and preach my funeral within 90 days. The leader looked around at the group and said that they were in a spiritual warfare in that meeting and it was "heavy" on the end where I was sitting.

Near the end of the service, the prophetess said she likes my boldness and stubbornness but that she will "beat me down." After much discussion, the prophetess told me that she would 'visit my house'. The Holy Spirit revealed to me that she did not mean to visit in person, but in a demonic spiritual way. Now I know and understand why the Holy Spirit told me a few days prior to this meeting, "In time of peace, prepare for war" and why He had sent the prophecy through Prophet Barr a few weeks earlier. In addition, the Holy Spirit also had me to put scriptures over all of the external doors of my house days before this prayer service took place. Anyone who enters my house can still observe the scriptures posted over my exit doors. I never removed them. (The prophetess could not "visit" me the way she wanted to—I was protected by the Holy Scriptures posted over my doors). God is so faithful!!

The prophetess finally ended the session by saying that God uses bold people like me and one day, God is going to use me once I get myself right and that God may use me even greater than he uses her {praise of Jezebel}. Please take note: The same way the demons knew who Jesus was and who Paul was (Acts 19:15-16), I believe this prophetess saw Jesus in me and knew who I was also. With God's help, I remained humble through all of this senseless humiliation. After humiliating me throughout the entire meeting, one of the attendees interrupted the closing and read a scripture from Isaiah 43:19, "Behold, I will do a new thing; now it shall spring forth; shall ye not know it...." I asked the prophetess whether it was okay for me to write that scripture down and she nodded her head in the affirmative.

The meeting started approximately 7:30 p.m. and ended approximately 10 p.m. Can you imagine the verbal abuse that I suffered? The majority of the prayer meeting time was used to humiliate me, so when it was announced to adjourn the meeting, I said to myself, Lord, what must I do now. The Holy Spirit said, "You love them." So, I got up and greeted everyone there with a hug, including that leader and the false prophetess. You can't imagine what it was like to hug and greet people who just got through verbally torturing you for such length of time. Everyone stood around smiling and talking as if nothing had happened to me. This was extremely painful, especially, after having been humiliated among people who I thought to be like Christ. Oh, the pain Jesus must have felt when His friend, Peter, denied Him three times and when His friend, Judas, betrayed Him with a kiss. And believe me, not ONE of those people in attendance has said anything in my favor nor offered any sympathy, or anything to help me through that ordeal up to this very day. Never in my life have I experienced such harassment, insults, and emotional distress as I did during that prayer meeting. Oh, what cruel memories!

Though I might not have recorded all of the abuse that I suffered, I had heard and seen enough that night to last me a lifetime. As I entered my car after the meeting, the Holy Spirit revealed the plot and plan of the enemy. As God gave me revelation of the night's incident, I was astounded. No one knew that I had the spiritual gift to discern that witchcraft was in operation at that church. I was distressed about the matter but was reluctant in telling my husband about the incident. As a matter of fact, I waited about two days before I told him about my abuse because I had mixed emotions about getting my family involved. And furthermore, I didn't want my husband to lose confidence in the broad-spectrum of church. Anyhow, the next day after that prayer meeting, I had excruciating pains in my head. Every time I tried to tell trusted prayer partners what happened, I would get sick immediately and the pain in my head would intensify as if to make me close my mouth.

Despite the pain, I felt I needed to share what had happened in the meeting. I said to myself that if I were going to die in 90 days, at least someone should know what happened to me. As I tried to express myself to a few of the people who were at that prayer meeting, I was told to keep my mouth shut about the whole matter. Oh, how it hurts to know that people wanted me to conceal the whole matter. I have experienced enough at this point in life to know, hallelujah, that God allows people to be placed in positions of authority, but that it is God who has the last word and ultimate authority.

I had finally met my Goliath in life—witchcraft. I fasted and prayed many days and continually confessed deliverance from my head pains and the depression that I was experiencing. I kept saying, "Why, Lord?" Eventually, I received my answer that witchcraft is used mainly to control people and to bring people into bondage. When people can't control you in the natural, they will try to control you supernaturally with satanic forces. The Holy Spirit said He needed to use me to manifest His power over witchcraft and that I had to experience the effect of the witchcraft to know that it was real and to confirm that I was in spiritual warfare. You see, prior to this incident, I didn't believe something like this could happen to anybody. Many days I fasted and prayed that my pains would just go away. There were many days while I traveled to work miles away from home that my pains would become seemingly unbearable. The Holy Spirit would not allow me to take any medication for the pains. Instead, I would anoint my head and my left hand as the Holy Spirit directed me. I did this day after day and it seemed I had become VERY discouraged since I did not FEEL any changes. Then the Holy Spirit spoke so powerfully to my spirit one day and said, "IT MAY SEEM LIKE IT'S NOT WORKING, BUT IT IS!" Oh, my God, what a word!

After that day, I became more humble and confident in my obeying God's direction to me. I called a sister from out of state to pray with me and I always remember and repeat her words of prayer when she said, "I CANCEL EVERY PLOT, PLAN, ASSIGNMENT, ATTACK, AND SCHEME OF THE DEVIL." When I prayed these words and repeated scriptures as the Holy Spirit directed me, it seemed like I gazed in the spirit realm and saw demons backing away from me. Oh yes, I was finally learning to fight in the spirit realm. I had to experience God's power for deliverance during this warfare. While fighting in prayer, some days I actually pushed my chair away from my desk at work and knelt on the floor just to balance my head on my body and to try to alleviate my pains. Yet, I had to do that very secretly to avoid a scene and pray for strength to finish the day's work. I kept answering the busy phone, I kept smiling, and I would be so glad when the day was ended so I could get in my car and cry out to God for help. Some days I called trusted co-workers about pains in my head and asked them to say a word of prayer for me.

One particular day, I had so much pain and was so stressed out that I asked a former boss if I was talking cohesively. I almost called my husband to take me to the asylum but the Holy Spirit stepped in and would not allow me to make that confession of insanity. Matthew 12:37 reminded me, "For by thy words thou shalt be justified, and by thy words thou shalt be condemned." In addition, Proverbs 18:21 declares, "Death and life are in the power of the tongue...." Instead of making the confession of insanity, the Holy Spirit brought these words to my remembrance, "I know that I can make it—I know that I can stand—no matter what may come my way—my life is in God's hand."

It is of paramount importance to understand that fear will paralyze you. It seemed the more pain I experienced the more fear of the unknown was developing within me. For example, when I went to the beautician for my next appointment, I would pray that my hair would not fall out because of the intensity of pain in my head and—my scalp was very sore. Eventually, I got to the place when I walked, it seems to me that my body was twisting and I found myself walking sometimes with a wobble, uncontrollably. Whenever I drove over a body of water, it seems my pains would intensify. I had no alternate route, so I had to drive over bodies of water every day to get to work, church, or wherever I needed to go. I would just dread when I had to cross a bridge, because I knew that I had no other choice except to cross the bridge. When I noticed the pattern of the pains when crossing water, the Holy Spirit told me to visualize all the water as the blood of Jesus and my pain would not intensify if I plead the blood of Jesus.

In addition, I experienced a constant nervousness in my stomach. The enemy tried to make me confess that a snake was moving in my stomach. There were constant movements in my stomach as if a baby was inside of me. I never made the confession of a snake being inside of me. Instead, the Holy Spirit urged me to confess that the Spirit of truth lives within me in accordance with John 14:17 as it declares: "Even the Spirit of truth; whom the world cannot receive, because it seeth him not, neither knoweth him: but ye know him; for he dwelleth with, and shall be in you." Also, First John

4:4 affirms, "…greater is he that is in you, than he that is in the world." I continued to confess God's Word and one day the Holy Spirit directed me to pray and swallow just a few drops of anointing oil. Shortly thereafter that same day, I expelled a jet-black substance and the nervousness and constant movement in my stomach disappeared. Praise the Lord! I could not tell people everything that I was experiencing because someone probably would have suggested that someone admit me to an asylum. Yes, Satan was out to drive me crazy and really make me kill myself in 90 days.

    I recall the Holy Spirit leading me to attend a deliverance ministry one Friday night. The Holy Spirit told me to just go and sit but not to say one word about my sickness. I REALLY needed to see what God was up to this night! As I sat in the audience partially enjoying the service, the saints discerned that I was tormented by witchcraft. The saints prayed, rebuked, prophesied, and declared that I was delivered from the evil. They told me that I must believe that I am delivered and that I must confess the Word of God daily, even if I continued to have pains. Oh, what a blessing it was to see the Holy Spirit operate through the gift of discernment along with the other eight gifts that night. It was amazing how they told me things that had happened and were going to happen concerning this witchcraft experience. They invited me back to their weekly Bible study and they taught me that I must use God's Word and let my confession continuously flow from my lips. I had to confess like David in Psalm 34:1, "I will bless the Lord at all times: his praise shall continually be in my mouth." Up to this very day, I thank God for His servants who ministered to me during this period of suffering and pain in my life.

Even after my deliverance episode, I continually confessed that I was delivered; but I slept with the Bible under my head many nights trying to find pain relief. I shared David's thoughts when he said in Psalm 22:2, "O my God, I cry in the daytime, but thou hearest not; and in the night season, and am not silent." Furthermore, there is a powerful Word in Psalm 56:1-6, "Be merciful unto me, O God: for man would swallow me up; he fighting daily oppresseth me. Mine enemies would daily swallow me up: for they be many that fight against me, O thou most High... I will not fear what flesh can do unto me...every day they wrest my words: all their thoughts are against me for evil...they gather themselves together...they mark my steps." I would be glad when night came so that I could get a little rest, but I also noticed that I was being attacked by Satan and had to do battle even while I slept. I would wake up tired from performing spiritual battle that I had just fought during the night. I would sometimes pray that the night would be longer so that I can at least get a little rest before the day battle began. Lamentations 3:22-23 inspired me when I read, "It is of the Lord's mercies that we are not consumed, because his compassions fail not. They are new every morning: great is thy faithfulness." Day and night, the enemy tried to 'beat me down' just as the false prophetess said she would do. I would hear things in my mind such as: "If God was real then why are you having so much pain?" Satan tried to make me doubt the very existence of God. Satan even told me, "If God's words were true then why aren't they working for you now?"

You see NO ONE in the church had ever taught me about this kind of spiritual warfare. So all of this fighting was new to me. I had only heard about 'putting on the whole armor of God' but to really KNOW what all of this meant was a learning experience for me. God, through His mercy, assured me to "wait on the Lord" just as Psalm 40:1-3 declares: "I waited patiently for the Lord; and he inclined unto me, and heard my cry. He brought me up also out of an horrible pit, out of the miry clay, and set my feet upon a rock, and established my goings. And he hath put a new song in my mouth, even praise unto our God: many shall see it, and fear, and shall trust in the Lord." I learned the hard way though, that not only did I need to sleep with the Bible UNDER my head, I needed the Word IN my head and IN my heart. And I also learned that I had to SPEAK God's Word just as I was taught at the deliverance ministry.

I remember praising God even when all I felt was pain in my head. Sometimes, as I would praise God, I would confess something like, "God as of this night I would no longer have any more pains." Yet the next day it was the same pain again, sometimes more excruciating than any other days. Then one day I said, "Okay, God, Moses stayed on the mountain for only 40 days, you stayed in the wilderness only 40 days, please let my pain be gone on this 40th day of pain." Still my pains did not go away, but I felt God's mercy because some days it seemed the pressure would be eased and I would say thank God this is all over. But to my surprise, it was not all over; many days, weeks, months, and then a year passed by and yet I endured the pains. It seemed the less I complained the more I spoke God's Word and praised Him, and the better I felt.

In times like these, I found out that we had better know that we are known in heaven and not just in the church because church won't be there to help you if your problem originates from within the church. In Galatians 5:20, witchcraft is listed as a work of the flesh. I know now that Satan does use this work of the flesh, but many people don't believe it and this is how they are deceived. As long as there is a Satan loosed on this earth, there will be works of the flesh; therefore, there will be witchcraft. Read Galatians 5:20 for yourself.

Only God can deliver and protect you from this evil of witchcraft. In my opinion, witchcraft includes dealing with evil spirits with the intent to cast spells on persons or their belongings. This can be initiated and be executed through praise, fear, manipulation, intimidation, and or control, just as Jezebel used witchcraft in First Kings Chapter 21. Remember what Jezebel did to Elijah and the other prophets in First Kings, Chapters 16 through 18 and also Second Kings, Chapter 9? Similarly, I was able to show instances where fear, threat, intimidation, control, and even praise were used against me at that prayer meeting. At that prayer meeting, I was told such things as, "If you tell what happened here tonight, I will roll you down the aisle and preach your funeral in 90 days. You are self-righteous and deceitful, etc."

I know that witchcraft is prevalent in today's churches just by using the ministry gifts of the Holy Spirit. I believe in my heart that I experienced what I did in order that I may help others who may later experience the same thing or something similar. Whether the church wants to accept the fact that witchcraft is prevalent in the churches or not, it still remains a fact. Just as Jezebel caused Elijah to pray to die, battling witchcraft was also a traumatizing experience for me. Not only did I suffer, but also my children were scared to go to certain places. It seemed for a long time that every Tuesday in the month, they would get sick or injured; their grades were dropping drastically, etc. Sure, they are only children, but they knew that there were drastic changes in their lives and my life as well. And through all the turmoil that my family and I experienced, we never received any counseling pertaining to this matter.

If someone had told me beforehand that I had to go through this experience, I would have probably said something such as: I would never make it through; and furthermore I would never be able to forgive anyone who would harm my family or me like that. But in order to follow God, you must forgive again and again. It may not be easy when your heart is broken to pieces and you occasionally look upon the faces of those people who betrayed you. But look at Jesus who called Judas His friend while knowing that Judas was giving Him a kiss of betrayal, He forgave him. Jesus, for the joy that was set before Him, endured all of His hardship and His cross. We, too, must keep our eyes on Jesus and remember that joy is set before us as well.

About false prophecy: be careful of the words that you accept into your spirit; test the spirit(s) to see if they are of God. When I recalled some of the words that came from the false prophetess, my heart thinks on Lamentations 3:37 which says, "Who is he that saith, and it cometh to pass, when the Lord commandeth it not?" Now, if I didn't know of this scripture, and had not received previous 'true' prophecies, I would still be suffering physically, emotionally, and spiritually—if not dead by now. But, you see,

God had prepared me for war. Please, please, please, read God's Word and try the spirit(s) by the Word of God.

I recall so vividly, one morning before my retirement, while getting ready for work, I was in so much pain, but was led by the Holy Spirit and knelt down at a chair in my bathroom. I had already had a spiritual battle during the night and the morning battle had already begun. In my mind, I was wishing that the pain and torture would just go away. The Holy Spirit told me that "wishing" is not "trusting." The Holy Spirit showed me where I was sitting in the spirit realm. I was sitting on my chair (throne) in heavenly places according to Ephesians 2:6 where it says, "And [God] hath raised us up together, and made us sit together in heavenly places in Christ Jesus." The Holy Spirit said as long as I sit on my chair (throne) and don't let Satan make me move off my chair, that "…nothing shall by any means hurt you" according to Luke 10:19.

This encounter with the Holy Spirit gave me strength and kept me in peace and with a determination to make it that day during work. My pains intensified this day but the vision or revelation the Holy Spirit showed me in my bathroom sustained me because I battled in my mind to stay seated in my chair. I actually stared in the spirit realm and watched Satan as he tried all day to make me fall or push me out of my chair. I could no longer 'wish' Satan would leave me alone; I had to 'trust' God to keep me in my chair where I rightfully belonged. I knew then without a doubt that all my trust must be in God in order to survive this day. I must truly believe God and trust Him to be faithful to me just as His Word said He would do. David said in Psalm 56:11, "In God have I put my trust: I will not be afraid what man can do unto me."

The Lord also dealt with me during this period of despair through dreams to strengthen and encourage my heart. My dreams were of utmost importance at this time. I dreamt almost every night during this season of my life and gradually started recognizing that God was actually communicating with me through my dreams. With this new founded source of strength, I had to rely on God's revelation and interpretations for my life. Most of the dreams contained my warning or instruction for the day. As a matter of fact, I had a dream about someone chasing me with a gun during the night. I got so tired running from this person that I finally stopped running, stood firm and confronted the individual, then proclaimed I was not afraid and would not run anymore. The person became angry that I was no longer afraid and said "You think you are strong but what about your two boys." The Holy Spirit revealed the enemy's plan and attack on my children days before implementation. {Who says God doesn't speak to us through dreams anymore?} Read the book of Daniel — messages through dreams are for real! In most instances, I wrote down what I remembered from my dreams and often asked the Holy Spirit to instruct me as to which dreams I needed to record.

Most of the time my dreams occurred around five o'clock in the morning. These dreams normally required me to pray and seek God for the interpretation. The interpretation of the dream would seem to be immediate because God knew my state of mind and that I wanted and needed His constant guidance in order to endure my pain. On a few occasions, after my retirement, I would nap during the day and the Lord would give me a word of encouragement through the daytime dreams. It is amazing what God allows, but it is more amazing how God helps you to endure what he allows.

Even though I had this bout with false prophecy and witchcraft, God never left me alone. I did not take any medication for my head pains nor did I visit a doctor for my pains. The Holy Spirit revealed to me that a doctor's records would have included notes of a possible nervous breakdown and could have been held against me for the continuation of my ministry. I can stand and tell the whole world that God is God and beside Him there is no other God. I can also tell the world that God will not allow anything that He does not purpose. Someone told me that God was so sure I could take the pain that He bragged to Satan about me and told him to take his best shot—just like He did Job. Well, while I was going through the pain, it really didn't seem like I was going to make God too proud. But, Bless the Lord, Satan saw whom he was messing with—you don't mess around with God's children.

On one other occasion, still in pain and being desperate for relief, I wrote to this certain television ministry and it appeared they had just the right answers that I needed for that period in my life. They would mail partial prophecies to me that sound good and I thought things were going to go well for me now. Each time they wrote me, however, there would be a solicitation for funds and a reminder that the subsequent part of the prophecy would be forthcoming. Of course, I was naïve about sowing and reaping my financial seed. So, I was learning to sow and didn't mind giving.

One response that I received from the ministry requested that I trace my footprint and send the name of my bank on the footprint. This act was to prove that I trust God for a return of financial blessings as I blessed this particular TV ministry. (Yes, foolishly, in a desperate cry of relief, I sent the footprint. My husband did not know about this part. Sorry, honey!). I didn't know that I was so vulnerable!

Then week after week there were strange, but simple, requests from the ministry. I was a little skeptical of this but then I recalled the scripture in First Corinthians 1:27 that says, "But God hath chosen the foolish things of the world to confound the wise…." I really felt very uneasy about responding to those requests but I was trying to be obedient to the prophet and I did as requested. Another letter came from the ministry requesting that I send a strand of my hair. I said to myself, no, enough is enough! When I read that letter and said "No," it seems a scale was lifted off my eyes and I concluded this ministry to be that of another false prophet. Just as I was thanking God for revealing this truth to me, I felt an excruciating pain in my head as if someone or something had burst through my skull. The Holy Spirit revealed to me that I had exposed an evil spirit and that he had departed from me in that instant of exposure. Thank God for His powerful revelation.

Witchcraft infiltrates the mind. It is amazing how people would play with your mind and your life in the name of God for the sake of money and control—even when you are in desperate need of help!! I never responded to that letter or any other letter I received from that ministry thereafter. As a matter of fact, I burned all previous correspondence; and all mailings thereafter were burned or ripped and trashed without even opening the mail.

Thank God for His mercy and revelation. Now you and I both can see why First John 4:1 tells us to "…try the spirits whether they are of God.…"

For those of you who are wondering what happened to the TV ministry and to those other people who harmed me—Well, I don't know about the TV ministry—I reported the latter situation to the district and state level of the religious hierarchy. Neither my husband nor I ever received communication from the hierarchy requesting that we, along with the alleged antagonists, meet to discuss the issue. It appears that I am the only person who was reprimanded—and that, in my opinion, appears to have been for speaking the truth. When I was reprimanded, however, my entire household suffered. Through all of that pandemonium, we made it and God is still blessing us. Yet, it is very appalling to see and hear of the things allowed in churches today. For example, it is repulsive for a minister to leave his wife, run away with another MAN, and then have his superior promote him to the office of a bishop. In the same sagacity, it is repulsive to have someone openly practice witchcraft in the church without being reprimanded by his or her superiors. Nevertheless, I do believe God—and I further believe that I am called according to His purpose. Romans 8:28 states: "And we know that all things work together for good to them that love God, to them who are the called according to his purpose." And David echoes a reassurance when he says in Psalm 29:11, "The Lord will give strength unto his people; the Lord will bless his people with peace." When I thought on the prophecy that was told to me—"This is your time of deliverance."—I held God to his Word according to Psalm 37:5 "Commit thy way unto the Lord; trust also in him; and he shall bring it to pass." I found out that some people would hate you when you speak the truth—just as Ahab hated Micaiah, God's true prophet (I King 22:8-18). So, hang in there when you don't see justice— God still has some business that He is going to take care of shortly. God knew how and when to handle Sodom and Gomorrah (Genesis 19:13). I know that He knows when He is ready to take care of business in these days. I knew that I did not have to retaliate because Deuteronomy 32:35 declares, "To me belongeth vengeance, and recompense; their foot shall slide in due time: for the day of their calamity is at hand, and the things that shall come upon them make haste." Romans 12:19 says, "…vengeance is mine; I will repay, saith the Lord." And finally, Ecclesiastes 12:14, declares "For God shall bring every work into judgment, with every secret thing, whether it be good, or whether it be evil."

God has a purpose for all that He allows and I firmly believe this. I believe Satan was allowed to come my way, not to totally destroy me, but to make me a better instrument in God's hand. I had finally met my Goliath in my life (witchcraft) but God helped me to slay my giant. I did not have any actual rocks or a sling; instead, my stones were wisdom and understanding.

If I had to make a comparison of my pain and affliction versus my new anointing, I would simply say that it was worth it all to have the anointing that I have now. I had power all along and didn't know how to use it because Acts 1:8 says, "But ye shall receive power, after that the Holy Ghost is come upon you…" Also, Luke 10:19 confirms, "Behold, I give unto you power… over all the power of the enemy…" I am grateful that God allowed me to be stretched and better prepared to serve the body

I HAD TO DIE EXPOSING WITCHCRAFT IN THE CHURCH
of Christ. I believe that nothing can happen to me unless God allows it and if He allows it, then all things in the end will work out for my good. He definitely blessed Job in the end!!

Chapter Seven
Another Sister Shares Her Encounter With Witchcraft

ANOTHER SISTER SHARES HER ENCOUNTER WITH WITCHCRAFT

As I prepare my manuscript, I am enrolled at Cathedral Bible College in Myrtle Beach, South Carolina. Here I met Sister M. J. who was born and reared in Brazil, but now resides in South Carolina and attends Cathedral Bible College along with me.

I had taken classes with M. J. in a previous semester but we never held a conversation. We only spoke to each other. This current semester, however, M. J. and I sat on the same row of seats. We both came to class early one day and she and I spoke and actually started conversing with each other. M.J began by complimenting my singing ability. (It so happened, she heard my voice among others during one of our Morning Prayer services during the previous semester). One topic of discussion led to another and I starting asking her about her homeland, Brazil. It seems we were destined to talk because M. J., to my surprise, had encountered witchcraft experiences in her church in Brazil just as I had here in South Carolina. She knew about spiritual warfare and the existence of witchcraft in the church.

My colleague continued to tell me that she recalled one specific incident when she and her husband moved to a new apartment in Brazil. Little did they know that this very apartment was cursed with witchcraft! M. J. said she found out later that a woman vowed that she would curse the apartment and no one will be able to live there. Since she and her husband did not know of this curse initially, they moved in with excitement and anticipation of a long and peaceful stay. M. J. recalls hearing all kinds of different noises on their first night in the apartment. She discerned in her spirit that the spirit of witchcraft was present.

M. J.'s husband did not believe in witchcraft and thus did not believe in the power of prayer to prevail against the evil spirit. My dear sister found herself fighting spiritual battles by herself. She said her husband's view on witchcraft and the power of prayer changed when he had a personal encounter with the force of evil. One day M. J.'s husband arose from the bed, as if sleepwalking, and went to their open apartment window of the 9th floor. M. J. said she saw her husband positioning himself at the window as if he was going to jump out of the window. She discerned in her spirit that she could not say a word to him at that moment. She knew for sure that she was in a spiritual warfare. Immediately, she began praying and rebuking the spirit of witchcraft from her husband and from the apartment. Prayers prevailed and as she approached her husband when the Holy Spirit directed her she pulled her husband away from the window.

She later asked him what was he planning to do at the window. Her husband told her that a voice down below was calling him and persuading him to come on and jump from the window. M. J. is convinced, and now so is her husband, that only God through the power of prayer prevailed over the demonic force and saved his life. By the way, M. J. and her husband were able to join in prayer and rebuke the forces of evil and reverse the curse that was placed on their apartment in Brazil.

Today, M. J. and her husband are residing in South Carolina as the Lord led them. They are both serving the Lord and declaring the mighty works of the Lord and His mighty power to deliver them from the power of witchcraft. Thanks M. J. for sharing your powerful testimony with the world and me.

Many people have lost their lives and many are still confined to institutions because they did not know how to handle spiritual warfare against the forces of evil. Some people fear being called names or being laughed at, or something to that effect, if they were to pray for deliverance from witchcraft. The fact of the matter is that saints are probably weeping because those people don't <u>ask,</u> <u>knock</u> or <u>seek</u> for prayer of deliverance. In some cases, I believe that the persons under spiritual attack have to renounce the power of Satan over their lives and give permission to the saints to help them in deliverance. When this permission is granted, the saints then have authority to command Satan to loose the persons and let them go free.

Yes, God is a good God. M. J. and I were destined to share our witchcraft experiences. Her experience adds validity to my testimony about the reality of witchcraft. When I heard M. J.'s testimony, I immediately

I HAD TO DIE EXPOSING WITCHCRAFT IN THE CHURCH

requested her permission to share her story in my book. I pray her story has blessed you as you witnessed the prevailing power of God's Holy Spirit. My colleague and I were destined to sit beside each other in class that day. M. J. has a discerning spirit and knows how to prevail in spiritual warfare against witchcraft. No one will ever be able to take away her spiritual knowledge on this subject and neither will anyone be able to take away mine.

Chapter Eight
The Battle Is Never For Nothing

The Battle Is
Never For Nothing

Through all that I endured, I died that my character could be developed. Character is not developed overnight. God allows us to experience different things in life. I want you to know that no college can prepare you for the training that God gives you on His battlefield. God can take the very work of Satan in our lives and use it to discipline us as needed (I Corinth. 5:5 and I Corinth. 12:7). Having read from God's Word, we can readily agree that all things really do work together for our benefit. We can rest assured that God does not allow anything in our life without a purpose or a reason that ultimately works out for the individual's good. Again, no college or seminary can prepare you the way warfare prepares you for future battles.

The Holy Spirit gave me a saying, years ago, while I was a senior on the Morris College campus: "Education without salvation equals damnation." That saying brought me back in line spiritually while I was at

Morris. Through that same saying, I found myself repenting and forsaking my own sinful ways and I was then able to put my focus back on Jesus. There is nothing wrong with an education, but what makes the difference is to know and to honor Jesus with your education. I love Acts 4:13 that says, "Now when they saw the boldness of Peter and John, and perceived that they were unlearned and ignorant men, they marveled; and they took knowledge of them, that they had been with Jesus." I want my light to shine that the world would know that I have been with Jesus, not which degrees I have earned. As you may already know, Paul was a very educated man but listen to what he said about his education, etc. in Philippians 3:7-8: "But what things were gain to me, those I counted loss for Christ. Yea doubtless, and I count all things but loss for the excellency of the knowledge of Christ Jesus my Lord: for whom I have suffered the loss of all things, and do count them but dung, that I may win Christ."

With all that was aforementioned, I believe the battles that we experience spiritually will be the foundation for our ministry and not necessarily come from our educational background. When we overcome a situation or battle in our own life, we must be willing to share with others how we have overcome. We should not be selfish when we see our sister or brother struggling with a situation and not offer any help. The Holy Spirit comforts us through trials so that we, too, will be able to comfort others during their time of battle. If Satan is fighting you, then you had better believe that you have something that he wants to kill, steal, or destroy. We must know the nature of Satan's work and know that he is real. The power of evil in this world tells you that Satan is real. Satan makes things look attractive, not the opposite. Satan is someone who has already been in heaven and he knows how to fight us. Satan uses principalities, powers, and rulers of darkness so there is no use for us to try to fight against mere flesh and blood (Ephesians 6:12).

We don't have to play Satan's game; we must do things God's way. We must therefore, look daily to the Lord for strength and power. We must remember also, that any weapons that Satan forms against us will not prosper even if he attacks us psychologically, physically, financially, etc. (Isaiah 54:17). We need to grow up and ask God to help us recognize the voice of Satan versus the voice of God. I believe that God will speak to us through various means, which includes circumstances in our lives. You see God knows our struggles and our weaknesses and will never allow more than we can bear. And through the whole struggle, I can agree with the saying that I have heard people around me reciting from time to time, "Our suffering should not make us <u>bitter</u> but <u>better</u>."

The TRUTH of the matter as I have heard a few people say: "We are stronger than we sometimes think we are, but Satan does not want us to know that." You see, my pains were traumatic, but it brought along with it an avenue for my spiritual growth. When you are weak and have God, aren't you strong? God will use the very thing that Satan is trying to use against you to help you to get where you need to go spiritually. If Satan could destroy us at his discretion, then don't you think he would have already done it! He literally tried to steal from me, kill me and destroy my family and me. When we stand for God, He will stand with us in all areas of our lives. I HAD to stand on the Word of God during my trials.

The Holy Spirit knows exactly which scriptures to lead you to based on the trials that you are going through at the time. After he has directed you to the scriptures, then it is up to you to believe the Word and stand firm. No matter what you see going on around you, you must still confess the Word of God in order for the Word to be effective in your situation. It may not be easy, but it will be worth every day of the battle. David seemed to have summarized my wilderness experience quite well in Psalm 31:11-13 "I was a reproach among all mine enemies, but especially among my neighbors…For I have heard the slander of many: fear was on every side: while they took counsel together against me, they devised to take away my life." Proverbs 16:7 states, "When a man's ways please the Lord, he maketh even his enemies to be at peace with him." Now, let me tell you this – God's Word works – but you need to be able to believe and let God's Word work in each situation. Remember, God does not allow you to go to war unprepared and without a reason. God is wise—our battle is never in vain! The battle is never for nothing.

Chapter Nine
Spiritual Death
Is Imminent
When The Spirit Lives

Spiritual Death is Imminent
When the Spirit Lives

We know that if we are alive on this earth that we must have had a physical birth at some point and time. Also, we know that if we stop breathing and never breathe again that we then experience a physical death. Death is inevitable!

It seems we can relate to the natural or physical side of things, but when it comes to the spiritual side of things, it seem we develop a "Nicodemus" syndrome. In John, Chapter 3, Jesus and Nicodemus were having a nighttime conversation. Jesus was telling Nicodemus about the spiritual birth versus the natural birth and Nicodemus said in verse 9, "How can these things be?" Jesus responded to his question and in verse 12 continued, "If I have told you earthly things, and ye believe not, how shall ye believe, if I tell you of heavenly things?" So, as you read further about my dying, YOU also may touch and agree with Nicodemus' question of "How can these things be?" and that's why I called it a "Nicodemus" syndrome.

Please ask God to open your ears and eyes that you may see what is being shared with you in this book. The Lord allowed me to see myself from the inside and that there were things that I had to die from (the wall within). The Bible tells us in John 12:24, "Verily, verily, I say unto you, Except a corn of wheat fall into the ground and die, it abideth alone: but if it die, it bringeth forth much fruit." While we know that Jesus was speaking of His physical death, it also reveals unto me how we must die from our natural life to live the spiritual life so that we can win others to Christ. We must die from those things that cause barriers to our blessings or promises of God to us. Of course, God is still revealing things to me about myself; therefore, I am still dying and tearing down walls as the spirit reigns in my life.

The struggle with witchcraft in the church was an eye opener for me and it was very instrumental in my spiritual growth, even though I did not welcome the experience then. I had to get rid of my self-life so that Jesus could be the center of my family's new life. I found out that in order to serve God and to be used by God, we must be broken (die). What I mean by being broken is that we must allow God to make us and mold us just as a potter molds clay. Sometimes a potter may have different uses and purposes for the vessels that he makes—just like God has different uses (assignments) for each of us.

God knows what it takes to make us and to help us stand for Him and He knows what it takes to prepare us to fulfill our purpose here on earth. Confessing Christ with our lips and not the heart is very easy to do. Living for Christ requires us to die from things that do not bring God praise, glory and honor. Many people backslide because they don't like the part where they have to be molded (die). We must deny ourselves in order to follow and please Christ.

God's purpose, the means He uses to accomplish His purpose and His timing are perfect; and they are always for our benefit. We have to be willing to be criticized, to be rejected, and to even hold our peace sometimes, even if you have to literally bite your tongue and say 'ouch' rather than speaking everything on your mind.

It is just so amazing what the Holy Spirit will reveal to us about ourselves, if only we would listen. Just when we think we have arrived, the Holy Spirit will reveal another area that we need to 'die' from. No, don't expect to have everything revealed at one time. You see, God has your best interest at heart and He knows just how and when to reveal things to you; He knows how much you can bear. Just don't ever look at yourself and think that you are all of that and a multi-flavored ice cream sundae, too. If you do, the Holy Spirit will soon remind you that you need some more molding and dying. When God allows us to be molded, it is always for our own good whether or not it looks or sounds like it at the time. Jeremiah 29:11 says: "For I know the thoughts that I think toward you, saith the LORD, thoughts of peace, and not of evil, to give you an expected end."

Although I will one day die physically and have a funeral, I am continuously dying daily as the flesh wrestles against my spirit. I can never say I have finally made it spiritually because I still live in this fleshly body. The good news is that the more my spirit lives, the more I die from the things of the flesh. I overheard a preacher telling another sister, "If you don't bow before God, you will not be able to stand up to Satan." Even Job did some spiritual dying. It is my understanding that Job had to confess his lack of understanding of God and also repent of his rebellion. In Job, Chapter 22, his friends thought God had left Job because of all of the troubles he was experiencing. But to me, it was only a time of testing for Job because when he stood and passed the test, Chapter 42 says God blessed the latter end of Job more than his beginning.

You will probably concur that sometimes you have to just tolerate the bitter before things get sweeter; and then believe that you will be a better person as a result of your molding and dying. God had to do some things within me before He manifested Himself through me publicly. My character had to be developed and is still under construction.

There are fleshly things in our lives that will not be a good witness for the cause of Christ. The flesh and the spirit are constantly at war. Therefore, the Holy Spirit helps us to get rid of these fleshly hindrances or sins. Galatians 5:19-23 states: "Now the works of the flesh are manifest, which are these; Adultery, fornication, uncleanness, lasciviousness, Idolatry, witchcraft, hatred, variance, emulations, wrath, strife, seditions, heresies, envyings, murders, drunkenness, revellings, and such like: of the which I tell you before, as I have also told you in time past, that they which do such things shall not inherit the kingdom of God. But the fruit of the Spirit is love, joy, peace, longsuffering, gentleness, goodness, faith, meekness, temperance: against such there is no law." Sometimes, dying to the flesh may mean for you to give up certain friends, certain relationships, etc. If you are not willing to give up these things in order to fulfill your assignment for God, then it seems you may not love God as much as you claim to love Him. It is amazing how much we love self verses how much we love God.

I really didn't know that I could steadfastly fast and pray until I encountered my dark days and nights when battling witchcraft. Oh, what a blessed time it was to be in the presence of the Lord. Listen, I am not saying that it is easy to stay up late, get up early or miss sleep at night to pray. It takes discipline; it takes dying to self. Sometimes, I would say to myself that I was going to get me a good hot breakfast the next morning and then the Holy Spirit would direct me to fast another day and then another day. The Holy Spirit through wisdom knew that I probably would have become discouraged if he had revealed the entire process to me at one time. So, I followed the leading of the Holy Spirit and fasted until the appointed time. I was not fasting for God but this process was to crucify MY flesh. I know that this process was accomplished only with the help of the Holy Spirit.

Sometimes when I'm not fasting, it's hard for me to go until noon without snacking on something, especially when I know that I have something readily available to snack on. So, I concluded that I was strengthened directly by the Holy Spirit. Have you ever wondered why the days that you are led to fast will be the same days your friends will come around and offer you the best of foods? Don't give in to that trickery. Keep in mind that God still requires obedience, even when it comes to fasting and prayer. If we expect victory in our lives, we must be willing to follow the path that God leads us.

We must do all things to the glory and honor of God. Obey God, and take heed that you don't think too highly of yourself and figure that you are so spiritual that you don't need to fast and pray. If you do, you may very well be headed for a fall. Don't ever trust in this flesh. When we obey God, we bring glory to God's name.

As I aforesaid, it was during my dark days that I died the most. The absence of friends was a constant reality during my dark days but that was time that I spent with God. Even the absence of friends turned out for my good (no gossip, no extra baggage, JUST PRAYER). I know that I had people who knew how to pray and were praying for me.

I was under careful consideration and scrutiny during the 90-day death sentence by that leader. Some people told me that they heard about me being in a state of insanity. Another said she dreamt about me and saw my obituary in the dream and she then became a bit concerned. Occasionally, I heard a few words of encouragement. After I had endured much suffering for a while, some people told me that they didn't know how to approach me because of the rumors they had heard about my situation. All of these different comments were told to me during the same 90-day period of my death sentence as announced by that particular leader. It seems no one really understood the profundity of words, nor of my excruciating pains—physically, emotionally, and spiritually.

I noticed, however, that when I needed to be ministered to one-on-one, it seems God would direct me to attend small church congregations who were on fire for God and didn't worry about the lateness of the hour when ministering to the needy. I had never visited some of those smaller churches until my time of testing. I don't have anything against large churches; I am just showing you where the spirit led ME during MY time of severe testing. It was almost compared to something like a teacher being able to give better services to a smaller size class of students. I also thank God for various television and radio programs that supported me in prayer during my dark days.

Yet, many times I had to continue to praise God even if I praised Him by myself. I hold on to this powerful declaration, "The steps of a good man are ordered by the Lord: and he delighteth in his way. Though he falls, he shall not be utterly cast down: for the Lord upholdeth him with his hand" (Psalm 37:23-24).

Chapter Ten
Real Living Comes After You Have Died (Spiritually)

Real Living Comes After You Have Died (Spiritually)

We don't always know why certain events are allowed to occur in our lives. But we must understand that whatever God allows is always in your best interest. We must depend on God's direction and take Him at His Word. God's Word always produces fruit and prospers wherever it is sent. God's Word will continue to convict sinners of sin and equip believers to serve in the body of Christ.

Jesus came and died to destroy the works of the devil (I John 3:8). In order to accomplish this, Jesus had to die physically and spiritually (for our sins). We, on the other hand, must die to the things that give Satan access to our lives. John 12:24-26 declare: "Verily, verily, I say unto you, Except a corn of wheat fall into the ground and die, it abideth alone: but if it die, it bringeth forth much fruit. He that loveth his life shall lose it; and he that hateth his life in this world shall keep it unto life eternal. If any man serve me, let him follow me; and where I am, there shall also my servant be: if any man serve me, him will my Father honour."

The more we die of fleshly things, the more our spirit man lives. My faith was being tried during my dark days, but tested faith develops patience. We need patience when we try to fulfill our destiny. I must let patience become complete that I may be matured and finished, lacking nothing. James 1:4 says: "But let patience have her perfect work, that ye may be perfect and entire, wanting nothing." We are kept by the power of God through faith. No one really begs for trials because they bring other guests that we sometimes don't know how to entertain, but faith tried is much more precious than any precious metal, including gold. Let praise, honor, and glory come from faith, which will magnify our God. God desires for me to receive instruction through my testing (my dying). Don't take your period of testing too lightly; and some folks may tell you not to take testing too seriously either. Personally, I take testing very seriously. But always remember we are dying to the flesh so that we may live in the spirit.

The more the spirit comes alive in us, the more the flesh dies. Hence, we don't really live until we have died, spiritually. We communicate with God through our spirit, so it behooves us to become more spiritual than fleshly. Again, in order to make spirit living possible, we must die to this flesh daily! Situations are allowed in our lives sometimes to create opportunities for God to manifest His power through us. Make up your mind to do something about your condition. Sometimes when God is preparing us for our assignment, it may be painful; but the end results bring joy to your heart. And somehow, you look back and say, thank you God, for allowing me to experience all that came my way. Allow the flesh to die and God can get glory. I died daily so that others may live—but who are the 'others'? Maybe one of them is "you" the reader of this book!

I have learned the hard way that it's not about me. It took me this long to die and still yet I am dying daily from the things of the flesh. Since I am dying daily, I will never have a spiritual funeral because I am continuously striving to be more like Christ. I am not perfect according to man's standards, but I am sincere and I am genuine for the Lord. Share yourself, your talents, and your gifts. Your gifts are for the benefit of another person in the body of Christ. Each of us is a potential blessing to another sister or brother. God uses you to help someone else in the midst of what you go through. After all, we do pray: "God, use me!" So make up your mind now that you have to die spiritually—the sooner, the better! **<u>Don't Play Dead</u>!** Keep on dying and each day you will get closer to life in Christ—you're almost dead!

Chapter Eleven
Guess Who Helps To Certify Your Death

Guess Who Helps
To Certify Your Death

Friends, friends, friends, and more friends!! Sometimes, with a lot of friends around, you may not take the dying process too seriously. No, you won't have a spiritual funeral but sometimes you might wish that this spiritual dying process would just end—right now. After all, you won't have time to think about dying with all your friends around, right? I used to hear my granddaddy say years ago, "Watch your friends, Evelyn, 'cause they all don't mean you good." Little I knew that I would tell those same words to others, not just because my granddaddy said them, but also because I learned the truth of those words the hard way.

I always tried to take people at face value. If they smiled long enough, that's all I needed to validate the friendship. But a day came in my life when I had to stand by myself because I could not depend on a friend to boldly stand on my behalf and support me when I stood for the right thing in the face of my oppositions. But I want you to know that I took my stand

and stood my ground by myself (of course, it was God who strengthened me to do so).

Always remember that you do not have to do wrong in order to get along and remember that it is all right to stand by yourself. Romans 14:12 tells us, "...every one of us shall give account of himself to God." I have had friends who because of their betrayal caused enough hurt in my life to give me something to write about. I can now relate to David's experience in Psalm 41:9 when he said "Yea, mine own familiar friend, in whom I trusted, which did eat of my bread, hath lifted up his heel against me." Again, in Psalm 55:12-14 when he said, "For it was not an enemy that reproached me; then I could have borne it: neither was it he that hated me that did magnify himself against me; then I would have hid myself from him: But it was thou, a man mine equal, my guide, and mine acquaintance. We took sweet counsel together, and walked unto the house of God in company." Furthermore, in Psalm 55:21 David said, "The words of his mouth were smoother than butter, but war was in his heart: his words were softer than oil, yet were they drawn swords." But guess what? We serve a God that mends broken hearts. We should bear in mind at this point that it was a friend who betrayed Jesus with a kiss. Yet, Jesus called Judas a friend knowing what his motives were from the very beginning.

I must acknowledge, though, that God will always have someone, somewhere, at some point during your struggle to help you along the way. With this thought in mind, I am grateful how God allowed a minister and his wife who is also a powerful minister to cross my path. They were placed in my life to offer encouraging words and served as prayer partners along the way. Their support was vital for my endurance during my struggle. These two people always offered words of encouragement to me and I saw how God took a bad situation and worked things out for my good. Bless the Lord!

We must be careful with whom we share our trials. We must ask God for guidance when we share things because not everyone who smiles in your face wants the best for you. We must ask the Lord to show us who is for us and who is against us. Sometimes man may not understand how God is operating through spoken words at a given time. Just like Joseph's brothers hated him in the book of Genesis, some people will dislike you because you tell your dream. Your dreams may sometimes intimidate those close to you, but you shouldn't let that deter you from pursuing your dream. I had to believe that I was representing my Savior when I was being 'killed' by my friends. Therefore, instead of wanting to seek revenge, I had to love the people who betrayed me. Jesus said in John 13:34, "A new commandment I give unto you, that ye love one another; as I have loved you, that ye also love one another. By this shall all men know that ye are my disciples, if you have love one to another." It is written in Romans 8:31 "What shall we then say to these things? If God be for us, who can be against us?" Psalm 118:5-6 say: "I called upon the Lord in distress: the Lord answered me, and set me in a large place. The Lord is on my side; I will not fear: what can man do unto me?"

Chapter Twelve
Living
During
Suffering Season

Living During Suffering Season

We as people of God must realize that whatever we suffer in this life is of no surprise to God. We must acknowledge that faith in Jesus Christ will help us weather any storm that comes our way. Paul says in Galatians 2:20, "I am crucified with Christ: nevertheless I live; yet not I but Christ liveth in me: and the life which I now live in the flesh I live by the faith of the Son of God, who loved me, and gave himself for me."

We should make up in our minds to stand firm on God's Word no matter what comes our way. According to the Book of James Chapter One, we can expect suffering to produce faith, patience, joy, knowledge, and maturity. I think my greatest hurt and disappointments (my suffering, I call it) came through those who I looked up to or respected in the church. And now, here I am, a vessel God has prepared and sent to the church for such a time as this. I am a vessel that understands the hurts of so many whom are suffering while in the church—Yes; I do understand the pain of many sincere Christians in the church.

We must not always look at suffering as if WE caused the suffering. I believe God allows us to experience different things in our lives. When God allows suffering or pain, there is a tendency—no matter how it comes—to get our attention. But think about this, would you rather take the pain or suffering that God allows and get your blessing afterward, or would you rather give up, be defeated by Satan and regret it for the rest of your life? I believe that suffering can possibly be used as punishment or correction. But, in my opinion, suffering may also be used as a means of perfection—but definitely an attention getter anyway you look at it. Sometimes, suffering can also open doors of opportunities. Some people will declare you should not do this—but, I believe we must ask God the reason for our suffering so that we will be able to learn from the period of suffering or testing.

Suffering seems to create an unspoken dialogue that gives us experiences that could have been otherwise too vague with mere words. I believe that God can work through us during our suffering because of what I read in Hebrews 5:8, "Though he were a Son, yet learned he obedience by the things which he suffered...." One of the ways to grow in faith is through experience. I know that the Holy Spirit is our teacher. Yet, I know the cliché says experience is the best teacher. What I am saying here is that in this life we will endure some hardship at some time, somewhere; and when it does come, with the right attitude, you will learn from your hardship—that unspoken dialogue.

Paul said in Philippians 1:12 "But I would ye should understand, brethren, that the things which happened unto me have fallen out rather unto the furtherance of the gospel." Don't give up during your suffering while the enemy is telling you that you can't take it any longer. And always remember that troubles don't last always. Satan doesn't want you to go through your trials. Rather, he wants you to stop and give up. If you give up, that gives Satan a victory and at the same time you miss a blessing. We must learn to endure our pain by trusting in God and relying on His grace. No one has to suffer everything or know everything, but God has people who have already suffered some things to help us along the way; but we must be willing to hear what others suffered and how they endured.

According to Psalm 34:19, "Many are the afflictions of the righteous: but the Lord delivereth him out of them all." When we are going through various trials, we are quick to ask the Lord to take the trials away. But as I look back over my life, I have to relate to Psalm 119:71 where it says, "It is good for me that I have been afflicted; that I might learn thy statutes." Truly, during my affliction, I learned so much about the ways of God. According to Psalm 138:8, "The Lord will perfect that which concerneth me: thy mercy, O Lord, endureth forever: forsake not the works of thine own hands." First Peter 5:10 says: "But the God of all grace, who hath called us unto His eternal glory by Christ Jesus, after that ye have suffered a while, make you perfect, stablish, strengthen, settle you."

I believe that suffering is only allowed for a season and for a purpose. I further believe that after the season of testing is over, God's way would have prevailed anyway. I had a season of shedding tears and having pains. I endured excruciating pains in my head as a result of witchcraft—it was very traumatic. Many times it seems I was going to have a nervous breakdown.

(Recall the prophecy in Chapter Six told me that the enemy would TRY to do that).

One day I was at the point of asking my husband to take me to a psychiatrist but God stepped in and gave me strength before I confessed and yielded to that satanic thought. I found out the hard way about the words from a sermon that I heard preached one day, "someone can take a man's freedom but no one can take a person's mind when it is stayed on Jesus." The spiritual arrows targeted for our minds come our way by Satan with the intent to destroy us, draw attention to the flesh, and/or to divert our attention from our focus on God.

As I mentioned before, God dealt with me through dreams to help me through my suffering. As God dealt with me during my suffering, He allowed His Holy Spirit to reveal the interpretation of one of my dreams. After this revelation, I started recording many of the dreams that I remembered or felt led of the Spirit to record. God kept giving me words or messages of encouragement during my sleep and I would be able to gain His strength and make it through another day. I have learned so much from my own dream experiences that I believe I have gained enough experience to write a dream book. Yes, yes, yes; God will help us and we must be willing to wait on God's timing and this in itself causes our faith to grow. When I read Psalm 27:13-14, my heart is encouraged because the writer says, "I had fainted, unless I had believed to see the goodness of the Lord in the land of the living. Wait on the Lord: be of good courage, and he shall strengthen thine heart: wait, I say, on the Lord." Yes, unless the Lord strengthens and helps us, we will faint during our trials.

I don't believe one can say that he or she is victorious unless there was a fight with someone or something. Your ups and downs (your fights) and struggles of life will only shift you to another level. Your unpleasant situation could very well mean that God is about to do a new thing in your life. Someone at church told me "My God can take the heat <u>out of</u> your fire or He can <u>keep you from</u> the fire—in either case, God is still with you!" It is not up to us to choose what God allows to come in our life. We must not become despondent when suffering comes, just keep supplying the faith so that God can keep doing the impossible for us.

When I think of the suffering I endured, I'm reminded of John 16: 21 which says: "A woman when she is in travail hath sorrow, because her hour is come: but as soon as she is delivered of the child, she remembereth no more the anguish, for joy that a man is born into the world." In the same way, I rejoiced when I no longer had to endure the constant head pains that lingered for such a long time in my life and the children seem to be back on track. It seems like I had prayed and prayed and had already passed my due date, but surely as the Lord lives, He heard my cry and delivered us in His time. Philippians 1:6 is also encouraging to those who may feel like giving up because it says, "Being confident of this very thing, that he which hath begun a good work in you will perform it until the day of Jesus Christ." Now get up from there and go and tell someone what God has already done and what He is doing for you!

Chapter Thirteen
Scriptures
That Helped Me To
Win My Battle

Scriptures That Helped Me To Win My Battle

"Thy word have I hid in my heart, that I might not sin against thee."
Psalm 119:11

As David found comfort in the Word of God, I, too, found comfort in God's Word during time of peace and during time of war. When you are going through difficult times, please relish the experience of hearing God speak to your heart through His written Word. The more you read and meditate upon God's Word, the more the Word becomes alive in your life.

READ FOR YOUR COMFORT

Genesis, Chapters 37-50 (These chapters address Joseph's trials and triumphs)

Genesis 50:20 "But as for you, ye thought evil against me; but God meant it unto good, to bring to pass, as it is this day, to save much people alive."

Deuteronomy 32:35 "To me belongeth vengeance, and recompense; their foot shall slide in due time: for the day of their calamity is at hand, and the things that shall come upon them make haste."

II Chronicles 20:17 "Ye shall not need to fight in this battle: set yourselves, stand ye still, and see the salvation of the Lord with you…"

II Chronicles 20:20 "…Believe in the Lord your God, so shall ye be established; believe his prophets, so shall ye prosper."

II Chronicles 20:30 "…for his God gave him rest round about."

II Chronicles 32:8 "With him is an arm of flesh; but with us is the Lord our God to help us, and to fight our battles. And the people rested themselves upon the words of Hezekiah king of Judah."

Job, Chapters 1-42 (address God's choice for Job to be tested and the outcome of testing)

Psalm 22:2 "O my God, I cry in the daytime, but thou hearest not; and in the night season, and am not silent."

Psalm 29:11, "The Lord will give strength unto his people; the Lord will bless his people with peace."

Psalm 31:11-13 "I was a reproach among all mine enemies, but especially among my neighbors… For I have heard the slander of many: fear was on every side: while they took counsel together against me, they devised to take away my life."

Psalm 32:8 "I will instruct thee and teach thee in the way in which thou shalt go: I will guide thee with mine eye."

Psalm 37:5 "Commit thy way unto the Lord; trust also in him; and he shall bring it to pass."

Psalm 40:1-3 "I waited patiently for the Lord; and he inclined unto me, and heard my cry. He brought me up also out of an horrible pit, out of the miry clay, and set my feet upon a rock, and established my goings. And he hath put a new song in my mouth, even praise unto our God: many shall see it, and fear, and shall trust in the Lord."

Psalm 41:9 "Yea, mine own familiar friend, in whom I trusted, which did eat of my bread, hath lifted up his heel against me."

Psalm 55:12-14 "For it was not an enemy that reproached me; then I could have borne it: neither was it he that hated me that did magnify himself against me; then I would have hid myself from him: But it was thou, a man mine equal, my guide, and mine acquaintance. We took sweet counsel together, and walked unto the house of God in company."

Psalm 91: "He that dwelleth in the secret place of the Most High shall abide under the shadow of the Almighty. I will say of the Lord, He is my refuge and my fortress: my God; in him will I trust. Surely he shall deliver thee from the snare of the fowler, and from the noisome pestilence. He shall cover thee with his feathers, and under his wings shalt thou trust; his truth shall be thy shield and buckler. Thou shalt not be afraid for the terror by night; not for the arrow that flieth by day; Nor for the pestilence that walketh in darkness; nor for the destruction that wasteth at noonday. A thousand shall fall at thy side, and ten thousand at thy right hand; but it shall not come nigh thee. Only with thine eyes shalt thou behold and see the reward of the wicked. Because thou hast made the Lord, which is my refugee, even the most High, thy habitation; There shall no evil befall thee, neither shall any plague come nigh thy dwelling. For he shall give his angels charge over thee, to keep thee in all thy ways. They shall bear thee up in their hands, lest thou dash thy foot against a stone. Thou shall tread upon the lion and adder: the young lion and the dragon shalt thou trample under feet. Because he hath set his love upon me, therefore will I deliver him: I will set him on high, because he hath known my name. He shall call upon me, and I will answer him: I will be with him in trouble; I will deliver him, and honour him. With long life will I satisfy him, and shew him my salvation."

Psalm 107:20 "He sent his word, and healed them, and delivered them from their destructions."

Psalm 118:17 "I shall not die, but live, and declare the works of the Lord."

Proverbs 3:5-6 "Trust in the Lord with all thine heart; and lean not unto thine own understanding. In all thy ways acknowledge him, and he shall direct thy paths."

Proverbs 16:7 "When a man's ways please the Lord, he maketh even his enemies to be at peace with him."

Proverbs 18:21 "Death and life are in the power of the tongue...."

Ecclesiastes 12:14 "For God shall bring every work into judgment, with every secret thing, whether it be good, or whether it be evil."

Isaiah 41:10 "Fear thou not; for I am with thee: be not dismayed; for I am thy God: I will strengthen thee; yea, I will help thee; yea, I will uphold thee with the right hand of my righteousness."

Isaiah 46:11 "…yea, I have spoken it, I will also bring it to pass; I have purposed it, I will also do it."

Isaiah 54:17 "No weapon that is formed against thee shall prosper; and every tongue that shall rise against thee in judgment thou shalt condemn. This is the heritage of the servants of the Lord, and their righteousness is of me, saith the Lord."

Jeremiah 1:19 "And they shall fight against thee; but they shall not prevail against thee; for I am with thee, saith the Lord, to deliver thee."

Lamentations 3:37 "Who is he that saith, and it cometh to pass, when the Lord commandeth it not?"

Matthew 12:37 "For by thy words thou shalt be justified, and by thy words thou shalt be condemned."

Mark 11:24 "Therefore I say unto you, What things soever ye desire, when ye pray, believe that ye receive them, and ye shall have them."

Luke 10:19 "Behold, I give unto you power to tread on serpents and scorpions, and over all the power of the enemy: and nothing shall by any means hurt you."

Romans 8:31 "What shall we then say to these things? If God be for us, who can be against us?"

Romans 12:19 "…vengeance is mine; I will repay, saith the Lord."

II Corinthians 10:5 "Casting down imaginations, and every high thing that exalteth itself against the knowledge of God, and bringing into captivity every thought to the obedience of Christ."

II Corinthians 12:9 "And he said unto me, My grace is sufficient for thee: for my strength is made perfect in weakness."

Ephesians 2:6 "And hath raised us up together, and made us sit together in heavenly places in Christ Jesus."

II Timothy 1:7 "For God hath not given us the spirit of fear; but of power, and of love, and of a sound mind."

I Peter 5:10 "But the God of all grace, who hath called us unto his eternal glory by Christ Jesus, after that ye hath suffered a while, make you perfect, stablish, strengthen, settle you."

Though I read many different scriptures during my battle against witchcraft, these listed above were scriptures that I referenced most frequently.

Chapter Fourteen
Some Important Things I Learned During My Suffering

Some Important Things I Learned During My Suffering

I have shared many things that I learned within various pages of this book. However, let me present some of these lessons in nugget form for your easy reference.

- Stay prayerful and watch; prepare for war in time of peace
- Keep God's Word in my heart and in my mouth, (not the Bible under my pillow)
- Be careful of my friends
- Don't seek praise from man
- Pride can be disguised, so don't get puffed up when the Lord blesses or uses me
- Be patient and wait on God
- God can indeed be trusted with my life when I depend on Him
- I don't always know God's timing
- "Wishing" is not "trusting" God for deliverance

- God will give me a word in my weakness
- Hard times will make me stronger if I don't give up or give in
- I must be willing to forgive the ones who offend me
- There are times when it seems God is not there
- Be compassionate about other people
- God will use those whom I least expect to help or encourage me during testing
- I must be submissive to my husband and others, as necessary
- Those who have been given authority over me can cause evil to come upon me
- I must humble myself
- Try to listen closer to "hear from God" and not man
- It's not about me, it is about God
- I have power to cast out demons
- I have authority that God has given me
- God granted me boldness, a fresh anointing, and a new dance
- The revelation of God is on the inside of me
- God is a God of deliverance
- Humility really does come before honor
- Everyone in high positions don't necessarily know our friend, High and Holy, Jesus
- Satan seems to target those people whom God uses the greatest
- I am effervescent about my ministry because of things that have afflicted me
- I have learned that <u>things could be worst</u>.

It is extremely important that we learn from our trials. Have you ever heard of students being retained in the same grade for a number of years? Well, maybe they were retained because they failed to master the lessons that they were supposed to learn and proved it by failing their tests. For this reason, I say to you, let us not allow our testing time to be in vain. Let us pass our tests of life and prove that we have mastered the necessary skills necessary to move to our next level and high calling in Christ Jesus.

Loyalty is required of all of God's children in order for us to accomplish our God-given assignment. Loyalty comes as a result of relying on God. The enemy can try, but he won't succeed in stopping you from accomplishing God's plan for your life, if you trust God for help. Satan will try to destroy you, or deter you before you get what God has prepared for you. Always remember that God will help you during your testing and or suffering; but at the same time, God wants us to be loyal children to Him, our heavenly Father. Learn to listen to God.

Don't rely on the hands of humans because they can't help you in the time of need. Read and obey Hebrews 4:16 which tells us, "Let us therefore come boldly unto the throne of grace, that we may obtain mercy and find grace to help in time of need." We must rely totally on the mercy of God. Let us read God's Word, hide his Word in our heart, and speak his Word.

His Word was sent to heal us just like it says in Psalm 107:20, which declares, "He sent his word, and healed them, and delivered them from their destructions." When we use God's Word effectively, then we can catch up, stay in step, and keep marching so that we will win our battles just like a good soldier of Jesus Christ.

Conclusion

Conclusion

"The Lord hath done great things for us; whereof we are glad."
(Psalm 126:3)

Time is running out!! We don't have time to listen to 'amusing' sermons that stimulate or electrify congregations for a moment. It is not pleasing to God when people persevere to attend church but are not being taught about salvation. They must be taught that sin is sin—and not taught that 'everybody is doing that now.' The Truth must be taught and then we will see spiritual growth in the church. People will know the reality of sin—the works of the flesh. People will experience the reality of being saved—and know that they must die to this flesh.

Moreover, people must be taught that practicing witchcraft is sin. Witchcraft, a work of the flesh, is prevalent in churches today—and welcomed by some, it seems. I did not appreciate being attacked with witchcraft in the church, especially among people who say they love Jesus. Despondently, I withstood the onslaught of Satan!

Although I exposed and reported the witchcraft incident, it seemed no one wanted to listen, not even church leadership at the district and state levels. Perhaps they thought it was futile to follow up on such a **SMALL** matter. Maybe—just maybe—when I told them about MY excruciating pain, etc., they were afraid of a witchcraft attack on themselves if they had intervened—I guess I will never know.

During the witchcraft attack on my family and me, I sought the Lord and died to many of my fleshly ways. As I died, I continually heard the Holy Spirit telling me to "HEAL MY PEOPLE."

In order to heal God's people, I have to give you God's Word. Based on John 1:1-14, "In the beginning was the Word, and the Word, was with God, and the Word was God. The same was in the beginning with God…And the Word was made flesh, and dwelt among us…" Also, Psalm 107:20 says, "He sent his word, and healed them, and delivered them from their destructions." For this reason, I offer you Jesus, the Christ, who was made flesh and still dwells among us through His Holy Spirit. It is good to read God's Word. Romans 15:4 declares, "For whatsoever things were written aforetime were written for our learning, that we through patience and comfort of the scriptures might have hope." Furthermore, I Corinthians 10:11 tells us "Now all these things happened unto them for ensamples: and they are written for admonition, upon whom the ends of the world are come."

You see, God heals people through His Word and I have supported the things written in this book with the Word of God where applicable. As a result, I have emulated what God instructed Moses to do in Exodus 17:14 when God said "... write this for a memorial in a book...." Dear reader, the information and scriptures included in this book will help you because witchcraft is real and so is false prophecy. I endeavor to continue exposing the work of Satan and help tear his kingdom down. God does not want you to be deceived by the tricks of the enemy. Satan is very cunning; he has lots of experience with his craftiness because he has been on his job and had others employed for a long, long time.

We as Christians must not only hear God's Word, we must act upon God's Word. First John 4:6 admonishes us to "...know ...the spirit of truth, and the spirit of error." We know these spirits by knowing God's Word. It behooves us to read God's Word and to personally know Jesus Christ as Savior and Lord in order to escape the wrath to come. Many people expect to run to the Bible, read a scripture in time of trouble, and expect to reap the same benefits as those who have accepted Christ into their lives and read the Bible daily.

The Scripture warns us in Matthew 7:23, "Not everyone that saith unto me, Lord, Lord, shall enter into the kingdom of heaven; but he that doeth the will of my Father which is in heaven. Many will say to me in that day, Lord, Lord, have we not prophesied in thy name? And in thy name have cast out devils? And in thy name done many wonderful works? And then will I profess unto them, I never knew you: depart from me, ye that work iniquity."

Furthermore, Galatians 6:7 says, "Be not deceived; God is not mocked: for whatsoever a man soweth, that shall he also reap." So dear hearts, be encouraged, read God's Word, believe and trust His Word. And finally, I use Matthew 7:24 to say unto you, "...whosoever heareth these sayings of mine, and doeth them, I will liken him unto a wise man...." Now I believe that many people will be 'healed' spiritually as a result of my obedience to God in writing this book.

As a final reassurance to you, please know that God is for you and wants you to do the right thing and die to your fleshly desires. Jeremiah 29:11 affirms: "For I know the thoughts that I think toward you, saith the Lord, thoughts of peace, and not of evil, to give you an expected end." I encourage you to make the right choice to serve God and take Him at His Word. Ecclesiastes 12:14 declares: "For God shall bring every work into judgment, with every secret thing, whether it be good, or whether it be evil." You see—someone who knows your every move is watching over your daily dying experience.

I often wondered why I had to experience so many troubles in life. We experience problems in life sometimes and want to somehow pray our troubles away. I found out that it is sometimes through our troubles that we are enabled to become mature Christians. As I think about my trouble, I realize now that I greatly benefited from the experiences that will continue to impact the rest of my life.

Now I hope you see the benefit of 'dying' and realize that just as part of the book title suggests, I HAD TO DIE. If I did not die, I would not have these testimonies to share with you. I share my testimonies with the intention that you can be blessed and become my 'fruit' for the Kingdom of God.

It is hoped that you are encouraged to believe that just as I overcame situations in my life by dying that you can also make it through whatever comes your way in life. If you are determined to serve and see Jesus, He will see you through.

Accept Christ and claim whatever you are asking for because what God has done for me, He will do the same for you—according to His purpose for your life. After you have finished reading my testimony, I challenge you to obey this command: "…and when thou art converted, strengthen thy brethren" (Luke 22:32).

God bless you for reading this book and supporting my ministry. Accolades to God, my Father!! "…For thine is the kingdom, and the power, and the glory, for ever. Amen" (Matthew 6:13).

SPECIAL NOTES

SPECIAL NOTES

About The Author

Evelyn Murray Drayton is an ordained itinerant minister and a retired accountant. She graduated from Morris College in Sumter, South Carolina with a Bachelor of Science Degree in Business Administration.

Drayton also graduated from Cathedral Bible College in Myrtle Beach, South Carolina with a Master of Theology Degree in Ministry. In addition, she matriculated at Erskine Theological Seminary in Due West, South Carolina.

Drayton resides in the Plantersville Community of Georgetown, South Carolina. She and her husband, Russell, have two sons, Justin and Nicholas.

Drayton has published three poems but <u>I HAD TO DIE EXPOSING WITCHCRAFT IN THE CHURCH</u> is her first book.

<u>Contact Author</u>:

Rev. Evelyn M. Drayton

876 Ford Village Road

Georgetown, South Carolina 29440

Printed in the United States
22332LVS00007B/112-114